The Drovers' Roads of Wales

The pictures are for Nicholas and Jeremy, Jenny and John, and all the many others who cheered me on through 1976, with love

The walks are for Daniel Louis Sayers

The Drovers' Roads of Wales

Photographs by Fay Godwin
Written by Shirley Toulson

Wildwood House   London

First published 1977
Paperback edition published 1978

Text © 1977 by Shirley Toulson
Photographs © 1977 by Fay Godwin

Wildwood House Ltd
29 King Street
London WC2

Designed by Ken Garland and Associates
Maps drawn by Colin Bailey

Photoset by Saildean Ltd, Kingston, Surrey
Printed and bound in Great Britain by Biddles Ltd, Guildford, Surrey

ISBN hardback 0 7045 0251 8
ISBN paperback 0 7045 0252 6

Contents

Part One   Prologue   7

             The Drovers   8

Part Two   Tracing the Drove Routes: the Welsh
             Countryside   23

Part Three   The Drove Routes   45

             The Way to Wrexham and Shrewsbury   46

             General Map   47

             The Way to Birmingham   136

             The Way to Hereford   149

Part Four   Epilogue   223

             The Drovers in England   224

             Preparations for Walking   229

             Welsh Words   234

             Bibliography   236

             Index   238

Acknowledgments

The research for this book was undertaken both in libraries and out in the countryside. I am particularly grateful to the librarians at the National Library of Wales at Aberystwyth, who gave me unfailing help and arranged for me to consult Dr Richard Colyer's recent thesis on *The Welsh Cattle Trade in the Nineteenth Century*, to which I am indebted for many of the routes south of Machynlleth. For the more northerly routes I am grateful to the archivists at Ruthin, Caernarvon and Dolgellau.

Several Welsh societies have given me enormous help, and I should especially like to thank members of the Offa's Dyke Society, the Kilvert Society and the Powysland Club, who have been most generous with information. I also acknowledge a great debt to the various members of the Ramblers' Association who checked the routes for me and informed me of any rights of way disputes.

It is impossible to mention all the individuals who have been so generous with their time in discussing the old tales of the drovers with me, but I must record my thanks to Professor E. G. Bowen of Aberystwyth, who has made a long study of the drovers' part in the social history of his country; Mr E. O. James, formerly principal of Golden Grove College of Agriculture, who has lectured extensively on the drovers in West Wales; Mr Thomas James, farmer of Cilycwm; Mr Showell Styles, who has shared his knowledge of Welsh walks with me; and Captain Sandy Livingstone-Learmonth of Porthmadog. Much of my information for the English epilogue comes through the kindness of Mr Donald Gibson, assistant archivist at Maidstone; Mrs Olivia Mills, who farms at Alresford, Hampshire; Mr John Thornton, vicar of Great Witcombe, Gloucestershire; and Mr Morris Roberts of Thame. If the information which these people have so kindly given me has been misinterpreted in any way, I must take full responsibility.

I have done all but four of the walks in this book. These appear on the following pages: 73, line 16-74, line 4, 129, line 6-130, line 9; 180, lines 1-14; 185, lines 27-32. They have all been discussed in detail with people who have followed the routes and carefully checked.

Shirley Toulson

Part One

Prologue

The Drovers

Long before the American cowboys launched a thousand legends, or the Australian over-landers doggedly took their cattle across a continent, the Welsh were driving their little black runts for hundreds of miles, over the mountains and into the eastern parts of England.

From the time of the Norman Conquest to the middle of the last century, any traveller in Wales might find his way blocked by hundreds of cattle, large herds of sheep, pigs and flocks of geese. From the eighteenth century, turkeys were added to the stream of beasts on their way east to the rich men's markets.

The traveller would not come on the droves unexpectedly. If he was within a couple of miles of a farm, he would hear them long before he saw them. It was a noisy cavalcade and deliberately so. The drovers, walking or riding at the side of the cattle, would give warning of their coming with yells of 'Heiptro Ho!' When the farmers of the neighbourhood heard that shout, they rushed to pen up their cattle, to prevent any unsold beasts from joining the drove to the east.

The memory of the noise the drovers made lived long. It was an Englishman from Surrey who told the historian Caroline Skeel what it was like. She recorded his words in 1926.

A great feature of the droves was the noise they made. It was heard for miles and warned local farmers what to expect. The noise consisted of the shouting of the drovers combined, I suppose, with a certain amount of noise from the cattle. But it was the men's voices that chiefly attracted attention. It was something out of the common, neither shouting, calling, crying, singing, halloing or anything else, but a noise of itself, apparently made to carry and capable of arresting the countryside. The horsemen and two of the cattle acted as leaders to the rest, and the men kept calling and shouting the whole time. As soon as the local farmers heard the noise they rushed their cattle out of the way, for if once they got into the drove, they could not easily be got out again. [1]

These strange shouts and cries were probably among the earliest noises that man made. Students of dialect believe that the words and sounds which have undergone the least change throughout the centuries are those which have been used in relation to domestic animals. These are the working noises of primitive man, handed down from generation to generation.

When the droves eventually came into sight, those travelling in the opposite direction were confronted by an imposing procession; and as the slow-moving stream of animals and their attendant drovers, mostly mounted on sturdy Welsh ponies, could stretch for half a mile, they often had to wait twenty minutes or more for it to pass by.

Drinking fountain at Golden Grove near Llandeilo in the rich, fertile valley of the lower reaches of the Tywi. From these pastures the herds started their long journey to the English markets.

It is not possible to estimate how many cattle were brought into England from the whole of Wales in any given century, but some round figures for particular regions have been recorded. A seventeenth-century writer reported that three thousand head of cattle went annually from Anglesey into England; and by the end of the eighteenth century that figure had trebled. At that time there were reports of six thousand cattle coming from the Lleyn peninsula; while further south the cattle journeying through mid-Wales to Hereford were reckoned to number some thirty thousand.

Each main drove into England would be made up of several hundred beasts. These large droves were made up of smaller droves from outlying farms and villages converging on a central meeting place. In *The Welsh Cattle Drovers*, [2] Dr Colyer quotes the words of the eighteenth-century drover/hymn writer Dafydd Jones, who likened the souls coming before the Lord on Judgment Day to the cattle converging on his native town of Caeo.

Usually the droves were divided into lots, and the drover who was responsible for the leading lot, often a drover/dealer, was known as 'the guide'. For every four hundred head of cattle there could be up to a dozen drovers. Corgis were used to keep the herds together. These dogs are so low on the ground that they can snap at the heels of a beast, and be well out of the way of the ensuing kick. They have great intelligence, and many tales are told of how the dogs used to find their way home to North Wales from Kent. Indeed, they could make the return journey more swiftly and directly than their masters. In the Ardudwy region around Harlech, people tell how the women started to prepare for their men's return a couple of days after the dogs showed up.

At the end of a droving season, the men's journey was liable to be more leisurely. Usually they formed groups of twos and threes and rode back the way they had come. Sometimes they sold their ponies in England and either walked back or, in the case of the more wealthy dealer/drovers, spent part of their proceeds on the public coach to the west. In any case it was a relaxed journey compared with the hardships of the outward route.

The clothes that the drovers wore for their work remained much the same throughout the centuries. Like anyone else who walks in Wales, they had to be prepared to face cold, wet mists and low-lying cloud, and to walk through marshy land. Professor E. G. Bowen of Aberystwyth, who has made a long study of the drovers, told me how they dressed themselves for their long ordeal. They wore the traditional farm labourer's smock, which, even in high summer, was likely to be perpetually sodden at the hem. To protect their trousers from the wet, they covered them with knee-length woollen stockings. These were knitted during the winter evenings in the farm kitchens, by both men and women, and sold at the weekly stocking fair in Bala.

The stocking was protected, in its turn, by leggings, which in the nineteenth century were made of good, stout Bristol brown paper, made somewhat waterproof by being rubbed with soap. Soap was also used on the soles of the stockings, so that when the foot sweated it slid along the sock, instead of blistering as it rubbed against the wooden soles of the clog. (The same trick, in a slightly more sophisticated form, was practised by Sir Edmund Hillary and Sherpa Tensing during their ascent of Everest in 1953.) The drovers' dress was completed by a wide-brimmed hat.

Even today most Welsh mountain roads must be treated with respect, and at the time of the drovers they were infinitely more hazardous. To the dangers of mountainous and marshy land was added – at least until the eighteenth century – the threat that the herds would be attacked by wolves. But the worst danger was from man. Brigands of all sorts lurked in the mountains and the drovers, who often carried large quantities of money, were the obvious victims for these cut-throat bands. Some of the forest lands, which are now wide upland moor, like the bleak desert of Wales to the east of Aberystwyth, were cleared to make the ways safer.

Because of the many dangers to be faced along the roads, any honest citizen wanting to travel out of Wales would join up with the drovers. The journey may have been slow, uncomfortable and laborious, but it was far from lonely. By the eighteenth century it had even taken on something of the nature of the European Grand Tour for the sons of the rich landowners, who rode along with the drovers for the adventure. Their youthful high spirits often gave some concern to the head drovers, whose responsibilities also extended to the boys who were sent along by their parents to take up apprenticeships in London. By the nineteenth century that responsibility could even extend to women. One of these, the redoubtable Jane Evans, who is commemorated by a plaque in the chapel at Pumpsaint, went along with the drovers in order to join Florence Nightingale's nurses in the Crimea. On some of the better stretches of road, this whole cavalcade might be followed by one of the rich cattle dealers driving in a well-turned-out pony and trap.

When did this all start? Professor Bowen finds a clue in his own name: 'Bowen' is a corruption of the Norman 'de Bohan', and the name's prevalence in Wales is an indication that many of the younger sons of the rich Normans who were given lands in England went west to seek their fortunes. They might well have used cattle to bargain with their richer relations in England.

In his history of Carmarthenshire,[3] A. G. Prys-Jones has recorded that early in the fourteenth century royal officials came to Wales to buy cattle to feed the household troops at Windsor Castle, and that during the Hundred Years War (1337-1453) the constables of the Welsh castles were ordered to buy up the cattle in their areas and have them driven to London, Southampton and Dover.

R. T. Jacks, the author of *Mediaeval Wales*,[4] believes that droving was a flourishing and regular occupation from the early Middle Ages. He bases this supposition on 'the number of men called Porthmon (the Welsh word for head drover or cattle dealer), which turns up in Lordship and Borough records of the fourteenth and fifteenth centuries.'

Certainly the cattle trade was well established by the time of the Civil War (1640-49). John Williams, a Welsh Archbishop of York, wrote to Prince Rupert describing it as 'the Spanish fleet of North Wales, which brings hither that little gold and silver we have'. It was an armada that was much at risk from Royalists and Parliamentarians alike. When hostilities started the gentlemen of North Wales sent a petition to the King asking for protection for the trade: 'Our cattle driven and sould in most parts of England, hath bin and is the onelie support of yo'r petitioners being and livlihood, among whom be many thousand families on the mountainous part of this country, who sowing little or noe corn at all, trust merely to the sale of their cattle, wool and welch cottons for provision of bread.'

The King's troops seem to have been more sympathetic than Cromwell's. In 1645, Roundhead soldiers seized nine hundred head of cattle in Gloucester, so depriving the eighteen drovers in charge of them of their livelihood. These beasts, all between six months and three years, were being taken to the English grazing grounds for fattening.

It was not until the eighteenth century that the English imagination was caught by the combination of black cattle and majestic landscape. Then intrepid travellers came home with stories of the sublime and awful things they had seen, and Thomas Rowlandson was inspired to draw a picture of the drovers.

Throughout the centuries the Welsh term *porthmon* was used to describe both the few extremely rich and powerful cattle dealers and the men who had the task of droving, or 'walking', their cattle to England. The vast majority, however, were drover/dealers, part-time farmers and inn-keepers, who did their own droving, sometimes with the assistance of unlicensed or casual labour. Until the nineteenth century, when the big dealers became more numerous, these independent drovers went round from farm to farm making private bargains, so that they could get their beasts on the way before the big cattle fairs took place. They also had the advantage of getting them at a cheaper rate than they would have had to pay on the open market. Often no money changed hands at this stage. Until the drovers' banks were established in the late eighteenth century, the drovers took the cattle on credit and paid the money after the beasts had been sold in the English markets.

This method of doing business demanded more honesty than some drover/dealers could muster. And as the farmers must have resented their dependence on the men who took the cattle off their hands, the drovers were frequently regarded with suspicion.

In Tudor and Elizabethan times, the situation was made worse by the ease with which the drovers could evade the stringent vagrancy laws, designed to protect honest citizens from foot-pads and thieves. This was altered by the statutes passed in the time of Edward VI and Elizabeth I, which decreed that both dealers and drovers must apply to quarter sessions for a licence to practise their trade. This licence had to be registered with the Clerk of the Peace.

A man could only apply for a droving licence if he was over thirty, married and a householder. No hired servants were eligible. This meant that those men who drove cattle for the big dealers had to do so under contract. Any man driving cattle without a licence faced a fine of £5 together with a term of imprisonment for breaking the vagrancy laws. A further statute, enacted in the reign of Queen Anne, made it impossible for a drover to declare himself bankrupt and so free himself from any obligation he had undertaken.

Another way that a drover could fall seriously foul of society was by carrying on with his work on the Sabbath. He could be fined for doing so, and in Victorian times this law was stringently enforced. The Radnorshire historian W. H. Howse writes: 'In 1845 three drovers were fined at Knighton for "pursuing their worldly calling on the Lord's day"; and as late as 1869 a fine of £1 with 8s 6d costs was inflicted on a man for driving a herd of swine through Builth on a Sunday.'[5] So you can imagine the drovers impatiently waiting for midnight to strike on Sunday, when they could start rounding up their animals for the journey.

This enforced Christian piety was often mixed with a more ancient pagan superstition. It is said that in the middle of the last century, Jonathan Davies, probably the most successful drover/dealer of them all, and an ancestor of a recent chairman of the Milk Marketing Board, would always pluck a leaf from the mountain ash tree that grew near his farm, as a good luck token for his travels.

However that may be, at one minute past midnight the work would get under way, and no time was wasted in preparing for the journey. The travelling started at dawn and the cattle moved at about two miles an hour, precisely the speed at which walkers are advised to calculate their time over rough ground. Journeying in this way, and allowing for some grazing time, the herds from Tregaron near the west coast of Wales took about sixteen days to reach Warwickshire. The distance from North Wales to Kent was covered in three weeks.

The drovers had to temper their speed with care. They could not afford to be cruel, for they had to deliver the beasts in good condition, so that they would put on fat easily in the English pastures. Cattle panic very quickly, the Welsh blacks quicker than most, and no drover could risk a stampede on a mountain pass. To drive these beasts over difficult country and for such long distances was an occupation calling for great skill and experience. When a drover applied to the county quarter sessions for his licence, like any other craftsman he referred to his trade as 'an art and a mystery'. In his case the description was exact.

The drovers' skill was well rewarded. The wages for agricultural labourers in nineteenth-century Wales were recorded for the *Welsh Historical Review*, vol. 6 (1972-3) by David Howell. He found that a man living outside the farm received 1s a day in winter, and 1s 6d in the summer months, when he would be at work from 5 in the morning to 8.30 in the evening. The man would probably have a family to support, for the younger men and boys lived on their master's farm. On marriage a labourer would set up for himself, generally in a mud-walled cottage, which he'd built in a day with his own hands in order to claim squatter's rights.

Compared with that hard life, the drovers did very well. Their actual pay varied from place to place. Professor Skeel recorded that a nineteenth-century drover from the Dolgellau area received 3s a day, and that he was given a 6s bonus when he reached his destination.[6] And it would seem that the dealers and top drovers paid for his food and accommodation at the inns on the way. The drovers of South Wales did not do quite so well. According to Dr Colyer the rate in 1830 was 2s a day for a licensed drover and 1s for his casual helper.[7]

Quite apart from their pay, the drovers were people to be reckoned with. Throughout the centuries they were always among the best informed men in Wales. Until the nineteenth century the few roads that existed in the country were impassable for most of the year, so there was very little communication between the scattered hamlets. The drovers were relied on as news carriers between the farms.

They were also the only source of information about events in the world at large. It was from drovers returning from London that the Welsh learnt of the British victory at Waterloo in 1815. Indeed, scholars still rely on evidence which the drovers reported, when trying to make sense of the disputed course of that battle.

In the eighteenth century, the drovers had tales to tell to the struggling Welsh farmers of the easy riches of America. Their reports started the Welsh emigration to the new continent. Those farmers who did not wish to leave their own country could at least learn about some of the new agricultural techniques that were being introduced by the English and Scottish 'improvers'. From East Anglia, the drovers brought news of the work of the agriculturalist Jethro Tull and the new developments with root crops. From Kent they brought cuttings of fruit, such as red currants, which were previously quite unknown in Wales.

More important than all this, however, was the fact that the drovers were entrusted with the nation's wealth. It wasn't just that the animals in their charge represented a substantial fortune. Many well-to-do families regularly asked the drovers to undertake financial commissions in London and many a rich man's son, making his way to a career in law at the Temple or the Inns of Court, would rely on money brought by the cattle men in order to settle his lodging accounts. Yet movement of cash is always a risky business in wild country. To avoid the risk of loss, the drovers of West Wales started an effective banking system at the end of the eighteenth century. Anyone wanting a drover to deal with a financial transaction in London put the money into his Welsh bank. The drover then paid the London bills in cash out of the sums he realized on the sale of the cattle.

It was at this time that the Welsh cattle trade reached its peak. The little black cattle that made up the drove were known in England as Welsh runts. They are now enjoying a new wave of popularity, for they do well on poor pasture. The old joke about their winter feeding is that they will put on fat from the ropes that tie the bales of hay which are fed to fussier beasts. Their other characteristic is that they are very restless animals. They require a large territory to roam in, and they can climb like goats. You will see them high on the mountain ridges whenever they are left to pasture on the open moorlands. So it is not surprising that the drovers were able to take them easily over steep mountain passes.

So in this way, from the mountains of Wales, came the roast beef of Merrie England. Today there is hardly a town or village of any size in Wales that does not have its Smithfield Street or Smithfield Square (the English term for cattle market) to bear witness to that trade. To the economist Adam Smith this was all a proper dispensation for the free trade welfare of God's Englishmen. 'The mountains of Scotland, Wales and Northum-

Pont-Scethin on the old London to Harlech road

berland', he wrote in *The Wealth of Nations*, 'indeed are not capable of much improvement, and seemed destined by nature to be the breeding grounds for Great Britain.'

So while the English squires and the English soldiers ate the beef, the Welsh farmers had to make do with a near subsistence diet. In 1794 the newly formed Board of Agriculture called for individual reports on the Welsh counties. Mr Thomas Lloyd and the Reverend Mr Turner included some remarks on the farmers' diets in their comments on the general state of the county of Cardigan. They found hard-working farmers existing on 'barley bread and potatoes, and sometimes a few herrings in the autumn when they are moderately cheap ... Malt liquor and meat are not within their reach.' And W. F. Mayor, who toured South Wales in 1805, observed that 'the poor Welsh farmer depends more on his livestock to pay his rent than on the produce of the Earth, which seldom furnishes more than a subsistence for himself and his family.'

It is now well over a century since the railways began to take over from the drovers and many of the old routes are long lost. In addition, new road schemes have confused many of the old tracks. Yet some traces remain. Whenever you find yourself on a lane or minor road which is flanked by walls or hedges set well back from the new metalled surface, you may suspect that the droves passed that way. The unusually wide verges bear witness to the wayside grazing that was allowed at some places.

Some routes have been obliterated completely by the invading formations of conifers providing wood pulp for Fleet Street. Others lie drowned beneath the reservoirs from which the people of Liverpool and Birmingham draw their water. In one area of central Wales, between Brecon and Builth Wells, one of the most famous of the drove routes is now a military training zone, intersected by concrete roadways.

Conversely, a few of the old busy highways are left now to the sheep, the buzzards and the summer hill-walkers. Such a one is the old London to Harlech coach road. On the whole though, the drovers did not follow the roads. They sought ways that would make softer going for the beasts, and by the eighteenth century they were anxious to avoid paying the newly introduced toll dues. The tracks across open country have now largely faded, and many of the old lanes and hollow ways that the drovers used have been ploughed over or choked with under-growth.

To reconstruct the network of routes that would have been familiar to any eighteenth-century cattle man is something of a detective task today. But it is possible; and anyone who wants to discover the old drove ways must be thankful that the drovers were in need of two things on their journeys: refresh-ment and overnight accommodation for themselves and their cattle and shoeing stations for the beasts. These two necessities have left traces that are not so easily obliterated as the old routes; and from these staging points one can work out how the droves must have travelled between the main centres.

As evidence that a town or village was once a 'main centre', people will quote you the number of inns it boasted. To take two random examples, it is reported that there were twenty in the market town of Tregaron in the west and eleven in the tiny village of Llandegla on the way to Wrexham. This seems impossible to imagine when one visits them today, but that is largely because of the inflated English idea of what an inn must be. Often they were simply farms which made a surplus of their own brew to sell to travellers. Even now many Welsh pubs share their building with a farm, and they are known locally by the name of the farm rather than by that given them by the brewers.

During the latter half of the eighteenth century cider became a popular drink in Wales, and by 1800 cider houses became common along many of the routes. Some of the old inns still have their wooden presses. A particularly good one is on the Herefordshire border at Rhydspence.

In the open country, a farmer who wanted to let the drovers know that he was able to provide food, accommodation and grazing planted three Scots pines. These were visible at a great distance, and the drovers used them as way marks. When they reached England, they found that groups of yew trees served the same purpose. These trees remain when all traces of the old inns or farms have disappeared, the stones having been used for other buildings.

Rhydspence Inn

Only the top drovers and older men slept in the dormitories of the inn. The younger men bivouacked alongside the cattle. This was not just done to save money. The men were there to guard the beasts and to see that they were adequately fed and watered. The cost of indoor accommodation varied little throughout the centuries, and for years it stood at 4d in the summer and 6d in the winter months. Frequently entertainment as well as accommodation was provided. Fiddlers came to the inns when the drovers were there, and there was dancing, and sometimes boxing and wrestling matches were arranged with the local farmers.

Field names, that fruitful source for the local historian, are useful in tracking down the sites of the old inns. A halfpenny a night per beast was the standard charge for grazing, and any 'halfpenny fields' throughout Wales bear witness to the fact that the drovers once passed that way. Sometimes the 'half-penny field' can be found behind a building which served the double purpose of inn and smithy. Traces of that use are found in the modern inns of Painscastle and Rhydspence, where the present-day bars are on the sites of the old forges.

Cattle had to be carefully shod for their long journey, and the shoes frequently had to be renewed along the way. The cattle shoes, or 'cues', were twin arcs of narrow metal designed for the cloven hoofs of the animals. Sometimes the cues were made by cutting pony shoes in half and nailing them on either side of the split. Cues of both sorts can sometimes be found today, buried under earth and debris at the sites of old smithies and in the grazing fields.

Even geese, who were also driven immense distances, had their feet protected. The method was to drive them through a mixture of tar and sand which would harden into a protective covering. In some areas crushed oyster shells were substituted for sand. Some smiths went even further. They would put a blunt spike on to the pads of the geese, sealed into place by the hardening tar. The result was that the birds would walk on short stilts. But however it was done, shoeing geese must have been a messy, fiddly and deafeningly noisy business.

Pigs had the best of it as far as shoeing went. They were given boots, little woollen socks with leather soles such as children wore. Professor Bowen recalls that his grandfather, who was a cobbler, made such things. However, as though to make up for the comfort of their trotters, pigs frequently had to put up with being muzzled on the road, a discomfort which would be very frustrating to an animal whose desire is to be for ever eating.

George Borrow reported in *Wild Wales*,[8] an account of his walks in that country in 1854, how he met some pigs being driven along the road to Llangollen. The one that was muzzled was of immense size, weighing about eighteen score of pounds. Not surprisingly it 'walked with considerable difficulty'. As Borrow watched a man came up and 'said something to the driver of the hogs, who instantly unmuzzled the immense creature, who gave a loud grunt on finding his snout and mouth free'. It appeared that the driver was the servant of the other man, and had presumably muzzled the animal for his own convenience.

Shoeing runts called for skill, strength and a good deal of courage. An anonymous local historian from Builth Wells, who wrote a short pamphlet called *The Trail of the Black Ox* about the droves in his area, explained the process as follows:

The work of cueing was done by throwing a rope with a loop which would drop over the beast; when it reached near the ground it would be pulled tight, drawing the beast's legs together causing it to fall. A man and a boy would then start cueing, the man nailing the cues on and the boy handling the nails; after the end of the small nail was screwed off by a little claw hammer, a slight groove would be made in the hoof with a file, and the end of the nail would be beaten into the hoof. A man and a boy could cue between sixty and seventy cattle in a day.

Although the actual shoeing called for speed and skill, the work that demanded almost super-human strength was done by the thrower or feller who brought the animal down to the ground. Men of some stature were needed for the job. In the eighteenth century a smith and his feller might charge anything from 10d to a shilling for shoeing a beast. In the thesis on which his book was based, Dr Richard Colyer quotes some of the contemporary shoeing costs. He discovered that in mid-century, even after the coming of the railways, a herd of 192 beasts were shod at a cost of £9 12s, while a thrower got £3 8s for felling sixty-four runts. [9]

Almost every old track, ridgeway path or hollow lane that runs between these inns and smithies would have been used for cattle droving at some time. They are not always easily found today. Only a fraction of them are marked on the Ordnance Survey sheets, and only in a very few cases are they posted with a public footpath sign. Sometimes the only traces left of an ancient track are the parallel banks some fourteen feet (4.3 metres) apart or more, still topped by the now gnarled hawthorns, with which they were originally planted.

The walks in this book mainly follow the chief cattle routes across a band of central Wales, from the Lleyn peninsula in the north to the south of Cardigan Bay. In the space of one volume it has not been possible to include the routes from the farmlands of Pembroke and Anglesey. My main purpose has been to show how a walker, starting off from various points in West Wales, can make his way to the east following the tracks that the cattle would have taken. Sometimes, in order to arrange a circular walk, some of the ways in which cattle or sheep from outlying farms would have been driven to join the main easterly drove have been combined into one route.

As Alfred Watkins wrote in *The Old Straight Track*,[10] 'My subject is not that of Roman roads.' Yet sometimes the Roman road made use of even more ancient tracks, especially along the ridges of high ground, and when that happened it could coincide with a drove route. But for the most part the Roman roads of Wales were there to link the north with the south, and the main cattle droves always travelled east towards Offa's Dyke. They went along ways that were old when the Romans came to Britain, and which were in use long after they left. Yet sometimes I have been tempted by a north/south road, which probably pre-dates its use as a route for the legions, and have followed it to link two drove paths. This is the Sarn Helen, a road which still runs intermittently through the whole length of Wales. It is a roadway laid, they will tell you, in the fourth century A.D. by Helen, the noble British bride of the self-styled emperor Magnus Maximus, who according to the tales of the *Mabinogion* was dream-led to Wales by the vision he had of her.

But emperors and armies are not my main concern. 'To conserve what is best in the Welsh tradition, we need to explore and interpret not so much the doings of the princely heroes or villains of recorded history as the largely unrecorded heritage of the people of Wales,' advised the Welsh geographer Estyn Evans.[11] His words apply to the visiting *Sais*: the foreign Englishman who may be Saxon, Viking or wandering Jew (I can't be alone in being a mixture of all three) who wants to understand this Celtic land. The drovers make such an exploration possible.

1 *Transactions of the Royal Historical Society*, 1926.
2 University of Wales Press, Cardiff, 1976.
3 *The Story of Carmarthenshire* (Christopher Davies, Swansea, 1971/2).
4 Hodder and Stoughton, London, 1972.
5 *History of Radnorshire* (Scolar Press, London, 1973).
6 *Transactions of the Royal Historical Society*, 1926.
7 *The Welsh Cattle Drovers* (University of Wales Press, Cardiff, 1976).
8 J. M. Dent, London, 1958.
9 *The Welsh Cattle Drovers*, op. cit.
10 Sphere, London, 1974.
11 B.B.C. Wales Annual Radio Lecture, 1973.

Part Two

Tracing the Drove Routes:
the Welsh Countryside

Tracing the Drove Routes: the Welsh Countryside

Derelict farm near Trawsfynydd

The mountains which form Wales and have dictated much of its comparatively recent history were thrown up 350 million years ago, during one of the periodic shudderings of the earth's surface. Their rocks have been moulded by natural erosion, glacial movements and volcanic action in such a way that every Welsh valley has its own peculiar, individual character. The result is that the Welsh scenery today, particularly in the north and west, is so outstandingly grand and beautiful that it is sometimes hard to envisage it as a working landscape and to interpret the marks you will be passing as you go along the old drove ways. For the most part they do not go by great houses or imposing castles. Two ruined abbeys, Strata Florida in the west and Abbey Cwmhir in central Wales, do come into the story though; and often the tracks pass by standing stones of mysterious origin and tiny early medieval churches built in circular Celtic churchyards. Perhaps there is a general rule that the more majestic the natural scenery is, the more minuscule and enigmatic are the marks that man makes across it.

Your way will pass by many derelict farms, and although these will look modest enough to you, remember that they were fairly important buildings in their time, inhabited by people who were very wealthy in comparison with those who dwelt in the now vanished cottages. Perhaps it is as well that the latter have vanished. David Howell has quoted some remarks made by Walter Davies, who visited Wales at the beginning of the nineteenth century and described the mud-walled cottages of South Wales as 'huts of the most humble plans and materials' and those of North Wales as 'habitations of wretchedness'.[1]

This book traces some of the drove routes through a wide band of Wales from Porthmadog in the north to Llandovery in the south. It is impossible to reconstruct the complete network, but I hope that walkers who follow the routes that are outlined here will go on to make their own discoveries. This guide is a starting point, and you can use it in two ways. You may choose to base yourself in one of the towns mentioned in each section and then make circular walks from that vantage point, or you could set off by train to the west, and gradually make your way back into England along routes that the drovers would have taken. Sometimes the main drove routes went along what are now fairly busy roads. When this happens I have tried to find alternative routes for you to take. For the most part, these follow the ways that the animals would have been brought from the outlying farms, either to the large cattle markets or to join the main droves. Where this is not possible, I have indicated how you can avoid the discomfort of walking along major roads by taking public transport.

Mountaineers talk with scorn of an easy climb as being one you could drive cattle along, and naturally the herds would not have gone along some of the narrow mountain ridges which lie near a number of the routes. However, from time to time, because a particular path makes a splendid walk, I have included ways along which the cattle would not have gone – although it is surprising what steep, narrow passes they did traverse. Many of the mountain paths were regularly used by pack animals in the Middle Ages, and when these are included in the walks I have indicated them. Essentially, though, this book is intended for walkers and not for climbers.

In the course of each regional section I have indicated the youth hostels that lie near the routes, and the drovers' inns that are still pubs. Many of these also provide reasonable accommodation, and where this is so I have mentioned it. In any case, overnight stops are no problem – Wales abounds in farms offering bed and breakfast or camping facilities. Charges for camping are quite often nominal – 15p or so – but it is important to let the farmer know that you are using his land. There is no common land as such in Wales, and there is always a ground landlord for even the most remote acres of hill and mountain, the grazing rights being apportioned between the neighbouring farmers.

This arrangement goes back many centuries; as the poet R.S. Thomas puts it, 'You cannot live in the present/At least not in Wales.' Here the past goes back a very long time, and is always insistent. For the drovers, as for today's walkers, it extended back to somewhere around 2,500 B.C., when the first people dared the Irish Sea to make the journey to the unknown land to the east. Some of them must have settled in the forests which now form the peat masses under the waters of Cardigan Bay, for echoes of their drowned dwellings are still heard in folk tales.

More tangible evidence of these pre-Celtic settlements is seen in the massive stone burial chambers, cromlechs and long barrows in the mountains of West Wales. Although these people were followed by successive waves of immigrants, it was not until two millennia had gone by that the Celtic iron-using people settled in Wales, built their hill-forts to safeguard themselves and their animals, practised a regular form of agriculture and laid the foundations of Welsh farming.

Many of the detours in this book are made because it seems a pity to pass close to some of the more dramatic Stone Age cairns and burial sites and not to visit them, or to ignore the traces of early Celtic settlements. A few of these places, especially the hilltop barrows or 'tumps', were notable gathering points for the cattle. Prehistoric men buried their great leaders on hilltops surmounted by a sizeable mound, partly as a mark of honour and partly to make a good sighting point, so that travellers could note from a distance how the route went across the hilltops. The drovers used them for the same purpose.

Quite often the churches served the same function, for many of them were built on the sites of places sacred to the Celts, and most of these are still marked by a circular churchyard. Many of these tiny, simple church buildings date from medieval times, and I have noted some of those that are worth visiting. Because they are so remote, Welsh churches are kept locked, so do not expect to be able to go in and walk round as you can in most English churches. If you want to see a particular church, you have to plan in advance and make arrangements to get the key from the vicar or churchwarden. Because it is not the usual state of affairs, I have made a note of those churches that you can easily enter.

Where these early medieval churches stand now, the Romans found settled communities of hill-farmers, practising advanced agricultural technqiues and using sufficient guerrilla tactics against the occupying power to keep themselves reasonably independent. For the most part the Romans settled in the valleys, leaving the original inhabitants to their mountain farms. Yet the network of garrisons spread across the whole country, and many of the drove routes pass by the places where the legions camped.

For five centuries the Romans and the Welsh lived side by side, carrying on business together and eventually inter-marrying. It was the collapse of Rome in the fifth century, and the invasions of the Saxon barbarians, which caused the turmoil and bloodshed that gave birth to the legends of Arthur.

Another five centuries passed and another great leader emerged, Howell Dda, the good king, whose codified laws (1150) give us detailed knowledge of Welsh life and farming in his time (915-48). The free tribesmen lived in family farms, each one being attached to a llan, the church with its enclosure, kept for the support of the monks from the neighbouring monastery. Howell's laws tell us how they conducted themselves.

Roman fort near Trawsfynydd

Much of the farming was done on a communal basis, and from the laws we know how these people worked, what they owned and what things were important to them. The bard, like the smith and the carpenter, was exempt from the common work in the fields, and any household which fell into debt had the right to retain two items: the cooking pot and the harp.

Unlike the Saxons the Welsh did not practise primogeniture, but divided their property among all their children equally. If this system had been practised consistently it would have meant that with succeeding generations the holdings would have got smaller and smaller until they were no longer viable. In fact, in each family there would often be one or two brothers who renounced their share of the possessions. Many such landless men became conscripts or soldiers of fortune in the numerous wars of the Middle Ages; and it can't be too fanciful to suppose that, even at such an early date, those who could escape the fighting satisfied their wanderlust by taking the cattle across the mountains into England. Even in those early years the trade was sufficiently established for buyers to be protected by laws which made it compulsory to withdraw from sale any diseased animal or any pig that had a record of devouring its young.

The patterns of medieval agriculture have left their traces. There are virtually no villages in Wales such as a traveller in England expects to find. In this land of scattered farmsteads there has never been a tradition of a cluster of houses round the village green. That lay-out grew from the open field plan, which was the usual pattern of farming in England from Saxon times to the eighteenth century. According to that system the villagers worked together on long, narrow, allotted strips of land arranged in open fields. Such a practice is only suitable for arable farming, and in any case is obviously inappropriate in mountain lands.

As pastoral farmers, the Welsh kept up a semi-nomadic existence for many centuries. In the winter months they lived in the farms in the valleys (the word *hendre*, in English, the old home, indicates the family base). Here, those animals that were not sold at the English markets or slaughtered off were brought into the byres. In the long houses, some of which still remain in a converted form, these were an integral part of the family dwelling. In the summer time the family followed the grazing herds up the mountains and lived in the summer farm (*hafod*). You will frequently find both these words in Welsh place names.

Old forge at Pumpsaint

Because of this method of farming, which persisted into the early years of this century, the sparsely populated areas of Wales continued to be organized in wide parishes around the llan. In some cases a few cottages might be built beside the church and the blacksmith-cum-wheelwright would probably have his forge near by, with the inn, often used by the drovers, across the road from it. The village of Pumpsaint near Llandovery falls into just this pattern. It consists of a few buildings on either side of the main road. A chapel has been added, and in this case replaces the church, and the blacksmith's shop has become a garage. There is also a post office shop. This is a fairly standard pattern, although in most cases the inn and the church are the only buildings left virtually unchanged since the drovers passed that way.

Do not expect to find more than this, and remember that many of the place names you see marked on the maps are simply farms, and many of these are now empty. Although it has been estimated that as much as two-thirds of Wales has, at some time or other, been under the plough, the farm lands you will pass through are still mostly concerned with the raising of stock. Only very occasionally will the way pass through the rich arable lands of the river valleys. The black cattle on the hillside fields are much the same as the beasts the drovers knew. The ponies that run half-wild on the mountains are the same types that they rode: the small descendants of the Arab pack horses, which the Romans brought over, or the sturdier Welsh cobs. The white and speckled-faced mountain sheep have the same firm wool on which the Welsh flannel trade was built at the end of the eighteenth century.

You can do all the walks in this book without going through the market towns, but most of them are so closely connected with the droving story that they are worth visiting; and, in any case, they make good centres for the walks in each area. The towns are given as staging points on the journey eastwards in each region.

Many of the towns in mid-Wales owe their size to the growth of the wool industry in the eighteenth century. Bala was the centre for knitted clothes, particularly stockings, made in farm kitchens during the winter evenings. Llanidloes and Newtown became industrial centres, with flannel weavers living and working in factories. Until that time all the towns in mid-Wales, even if they came into being as military strongholds, like Llandovery, had owed their continued existence to their importance as agricultural markets.

From the eighteenth century, the quarry towns of Wales also started to grow, but most of these are far to the north or south of the area in which our story takes place.

Dolgellau and Machynlleth are the most important northerly towns in this book. In the early years of the fifteenth century,

Owen Glendower held a parliament in both these places. But even at that time, their main importance came from the sheep and cattle fairs that were held there every spring and autumn. In the west the most flourishing towns were Tregaron and Lampeter.

The towns existed with the sole purpose of providing services to the local farmers and none of them grew very large. Many have dwindled into villages today. They are fairly regularly dispersed throughout the country, separated from each other by about a dozen miles, so that each farmer could comfortably get his beast into one market or the other in a day's droving.

The mud tracks which linked the towns were often simply the ways across open country along which the beasts had been driven. Until road improvement schemes started in the eighteenth century, with the formation of the Turnpike Trusts, they were impassable for wheeled traffic for most of the year. The cattle for the English markets were usually bought by the drover/dealers in the early summer markets, and brought into Essex and Kent to be fattened for the Michaelmas fairs. This meant that they were on the move during the summer months, so the countryside that you will experience on your walks will be similar in many ways to that through which the drovers passed. Three major changes, however, have taken place. The first concerns the traffic, for now that so many of the mountain tracks have been made into roads, you can't hope for more than half a day's walking without meeting cars. Secondly, reservoirs now flood the valleys through which many of the old drove routes ran and have become great tourist attractions. Lastly, there are now massive plantations of conifers, offering the heavy scent of pines in warm weather.

Buildings too have changed. The prosperous farms that the drovers knew have often become ruins. Cattle pens and sheep folds have lost their walls as their stones have been used for other buildings; and several of the old inns in lonely mountain areas are now no more than small hillocks set among surprising patches of fertile ground on barren hillsides. These bright green half-acres indicate old halfpenny fields, where the cattle were put to graze overnight and which therefore received a heavy

31

manuring. Most of the inn-keepers were also farmers, and you will still find pubs that share farm buildings, such as the Talgarth Inn outside Llandovery (see page 209).

The actual surfaces under your feet will usually be quite different to the ones that the drovers trod. Most of the old roads have either been made up with metallic surfaces or have degenerated into paths that sometimes seem no more than shadows on the hillsides. Occasionally, however, you will come

upon short stretches of a 'green lane', or a piece of track that still bears signs that the droves went that way. The old path will be about fourteen feet (4.3 metres) wide and will have low banks on either side of it. It may bear traces of once having been paved.

Two features of the countryside that the drovers would find unaltered are the hedges and stone walls. The Welsh take great pride in their hedging and even now, despite the convenience of posts and wire and the high labour costs of proper hedging, you will find beautifully made hedges, especially in Powys. The hawthorn hedges of the English countryside are largely missing, since these were made when the old open fields of England became enclosed, a development which did not occur in Wales. When you do meet hawthorn in Wales, it has usually been allowed to grow into a full size May tree, and you will often come across a row of these planted along a dividing bank. Sometimes the hedges coincided with parish boundaries, but usually they indicate the valley fields of the winter farms.

A rough estimation of the age of a hedge is to allow a century for each plant species you find established in it. In many landscapes the hedge will be by far the oldest man-made object to be seen. Methods of laying hedges have varied little with the generations; it is a highly skilled craft, and one that takes years of experience to perfect. John Clark, who wrote a memorandum on the state of agriculture in Breconshire in 1794, considered that the hedges (which he sometimes refers to as fences) in the Talgarth and Usk areas were so fine that they should serve as a model for other parts of the country. His advice on how to set about laying a similar hedge went as follows:

When a new fence is to be made, any kinds of underwood that can be most easily had, are grubbed up with the roots any time from November to March. These are immediately planted where the new hedge is meant to be made. Four feet is left for the foundation of the bank, the quicks being planted in the centre. A ditch is then dug on each side of the bank, and the earth thrown up to form this bank for three feet high, when it terminates in a ridge from 15 to 18 inches.

If the quicks can be had five feet in length, there will be two feet

Drove road near Painscastle

above the top of the bank when finished, but as this cannot always be the case, one foot above the top of the bank will soon make a good fence. The closer the plants are placed, the better; at least the sooner will the fence be impregnable. The distance between the circumference of each plant, however, ought not to be more than six inches. One row will be sufficient for these large plants.

Although you are not likely to see any new hedges, you will see a good many that were originally made to John Clark's

specifications. If you visit the country in the early months of the year, you will see the old hedges being laid for the coming year, with new growths being woven either between stakes or 'quicks', living plants, which serve the double function of acting as stakes and forming part of the hedge. The skill lies in weaving the living branches without twisting them too much, but at the same time seeing to it that they are bent enough to grip the stakes. 'When you're laying a hedge you're not making a basket,' as Robert Gibbings learnt from a long-experienced hedger in Llangurig, during a conversation which he recalled in *Coming down the Wye*.[2]

As you go north you will find hedges replaced by stone walls, often the only evidence that man has ever settled in this wild country. Like hedges, many walls are very old indeed. It is

believed that a few of them date from prehistoric times, and
that they mark divisions of grazing rights that were settled
centuries ago.

Like hedging, dry stone walling is a craft that demands great
patience and skill. In the walls that have been kept in good
repair, stiles have sometimes been incorporated and little
arched tunnels have been left, so that sheep (but not cattle) can
get through the wall. Sometimes a very narrow break will be left
in the wall, to serve the same purpose.

One of the greatest pleasures is to watch dogs working sheep on
these mountainsides. Because of the nature of the landscapes,
you will find that you can watch every detail of this activity,
even from a couple of miles away. If you make these walks in

Mr Williams's farm at Pen-twyn

June and July, you will frequently come across flocks being rounded up for shearing.

Although there are firms of itinerant shearers who go around the farms on a contract basis, many farmers in North and West Wales still arrange their shearings according to the old style, although the equipment they use is modern enough. Traditionally the communal shearing is one of the neighbourhood activities, without which it would have been impossible to keep

a farm going in such sparsely populated country. Usually, four
or five farmers visit each other's farms in turn, to help with the
shearing. Like harvesting this has to be done to a tight schedule,
so the work often goes on late into the night. Like harvesting
too, the whole thing can be thrown by the weather, for it's not
possible to shear a wet sheep. In the old days the shearing of all
the sheep from a group of farms was often done at a central
point in the mountains, but this is very rarely the practice now.

In the isolated upland valleys you will find traces of man's struggle with the land in the mounds of old drainage systems. One of the sad results of the recent accelerated depopulation of the valleys of central Wales has been that acres, which carried a good hay crop only ten years ago, have now reverted to marsh. This affects you as a walker, for many of the old routes now lie across country which is virtually impassable in wet weather. In the final section of the book I suggest some ways in which you can cope with very boggy ground.

The sad fact is that much of the Welsh countryside is scarred. As some farming communities turned to the sea for a second livelihood, the Welsh turned to their mountains. Gold, lead, granite and slate have all been torn out of these hillsides, as well as coal and anthracite. But even these industries are fast dying out, and in some ways that must be a good thing. On your walks you will pass old disused quarries of various sorts, and when you do you will frequently find that the landscape is dominated by bleak, empty barracks. In these forbidding buildings boys and men, who were no longer able to scratch a living from the farms, spent six days of the week, while they risked their lives at quarrying.

Disused quarry

Yet the countryside is not simply an archive for the historian and the tourist. The farmers who graze their livestock here today are making a living in ways that the old drovers would be able to understand, even if the modern techniques seemed strange. What would really bewilder them would be the overhead electricity cables, the pine trees, the craft shops and the activities of the many adventure centres, which have been set up in the mountains.

1   *Welsh Historical Review*, vol. 6, 1972/3.
2   Temple Press, Letchworth, 1942.

Part Three

The Drove Routes

The Way to Wrexham and Shrewsbury

The northern drove routes that are described in this book cross some of the most dramatic ranges of the mountainous heartland of Wales. Before they reached the Cheshire and Shropshire plains, all the cattle had to go over three distinct highland regions. Six such areas are covered in this section, for we are going to tackle two parallel routes.

Starting from the west, the northern route goes through the southern passes of Snowdonia, into which the cattle were forced by the tidal sand flats which formed the wide Glaslyn estuary before nineteenth-century engineers built embankments and drained the marshes. To the south of those marshes, the cattle went across the rugged mountains that form the eastern edge of the Harlech dome, and the gentler ones to the south which face the dramatic massif of Cader Idris and the wide estuary of Mawddach, with Dolgellau at its head.

In the north, these western mountains contain useful mineral deposits; by the mid-eighteenth century the slate quarries, which were to flourish for two hundred years, were fully working, and some of the old drove routes must have been shared by the quarrymen. Today the deserted quarry workings and the ruined barracks where the workers lived are ghost villages, transected by rough paths that are left to the holiday walkers.

When they reached the Vale of Ffestiniog, the beasts that were bound for Wrexham had to climb on to the high marsh of the Migneint to the east. Those that had crossed from Harlech to Trawsfynydd and Dolgellau went over the mountainous waste

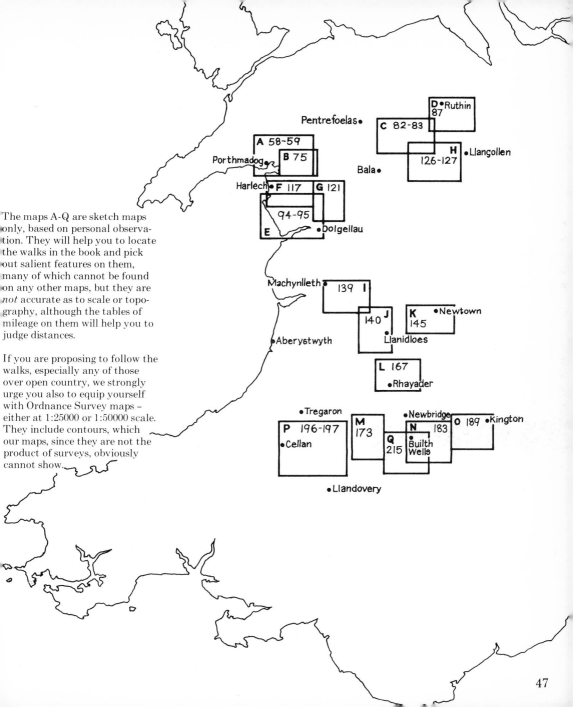

The maps A-Q are sketch maps only. They will help you to locate the walks in the book and pick out salient features on them, many of which cannot be found on any other maps, but they are *not* accurate as to scale or topography, although the tables of mileage on them will help you to judge distances.

If you are proposing to follow the walks, especially any of those over open country, we strongly urge you also to equip yourself with Ordnance Survey maps – either at 1:25000 or 1:50000 scale. They include contours, which our maps, since they are not the product of surveys, obviously cannot show.

Pentrefoelas•

D •Ruthin
87

C 82-83

A 58-59

B 75

Porthmadog•

H •Llangollen
126-127

Bala•

Harlech• F 117 G 121

94-95

E •Dolgellau

Machynlleth• 139 I

140 J

K •Newtown
145

•Aberystwyth

Llanidloes•

L 167

•Rhayader

•Tregaron

•Newbridge

O 189 •Kington

P 196-197

M 173

N 183

•Cellan

Q 215

Builth Wells•

•Llandovery

47

land to Bala, across land which is covered in bracken, gorse and heather, and which is intersected by wide peat bogs.

Both routes converge along the steep valleys of the Alwen and the Dee, along which the busy A5 now runs. From here they had to climb again. The beasts for the north went towards Ruthin and over the Clwydian range, with its deposits of lead and zinc and the quarrying area around Llanarmon-yn-Ial. Those that were heading for Oswestry and Shrewsbury climbed south and east from the Dee valley and went over the Berwyn to the beautiful vale of Ceiriog.

Roman road at Ceiriog

Porthmadog

(Ordnance Survey sheets 123/115/124/116/117)

Many of the black cattle that travelled east across North Wales came from the rich grazing lands of Anglesey, the nurturing mother of Wales. Until Thomas Telford built the Menai Suspension Bridge in 1826, the animals had to start their journey with a dramatic swim across the narrow but turbulent stretch of water that cuts Anglesey off from the mainland. Many must have been drowned before the start of the trek east, yet throughout the seventeenth and eighteenth centuries the trade flourished.

The eighteenth-century drovers from this area owe their immortality to a landowner, Mr William Bulkeley of Brynddu, a man noted for his Whig politics, who happily for posterity kept a fairly detailed diary of the middle years of the century. On April 10th, 1734, he recorded that he wrote to the drover Thomas Lewis, asking him to 'pay for my son (who is clerk to Mr Richard Eadnell in Southampton Buildings, Chancery Lane, London) fifteen pounds, part of which, about five pounds, he is to pay to Mr Eadnell what he laid out in entertaining his student at the Inner Temple at Candlemass last, the rest he is to take to his own use.'

Not all Mr Bulkeley's drover acquaintances were so reliable. Droving attracted as many rascals as any other trade, and Richard Hughes of Cefn appears to have been one of them. Mr Bulkeley wrote about him as 'ye drover who this session hath a tryall at Common Law besides a suit in Chancery against him. I told Mr John Owen that if his friendship to Cousin Morgan were real he would not countenance such a scrum as Richard Hughes to plague a gentleman as he did.'

Throughout the centuries the cattle trade remained the main concern of the men of the island of Anglesey. And it is no wonder that the drover immortalized by George Borrow as Bos should have taken that busybody travel writer for a cattle dealer: 'I can't conceive how any person, either gentle or simple, could have any business in Anglesey save that business was pigs or cattle,' he told the indignant author, when he visited Wales in 1854. Borrow's scorn of the drovers must have arisen out of one of the many unshakeable prejudices to which he was prone. Yet he does have the grace to record that Bos was not an unlettered man; he had been to school in Beaumaris, was much admired among his fellows, and was considered to be 'the cutest man in these parts'.[1]

The Lleyn peninsula was another rich source of cattle for the English markets, and three thousand black runts were driven east from there each year.

Here the interesting walking country lies in the mountainous north, where the Iron Age hill-forts stand. However, if you want to follow the route of the cattle from the very north-westerly tip of Wales, you could take the train to Pwllheli and from there go by bus to Aberdaron, on whose sandy beaches the cattle from the holy island of Bardsey would have landed for their journey to market. Yet Aberdaron was perhaps better known as a centre for pilgrims rather than for cattle. From this village (whose vicar is the poet R. S. Thomas) you can start your journey to the east by eating in the kitchen which was originally set up on the waterside in 1300, for the rest and refreshment of pilgrims visiting the saints of Bardsey.

During his Welsh travels, the eighteenth-century writer Thomas Pennant visited Lleyn and found that 'notwithstanding the laudable example of the gentry, the country is in an unimproved state, neglected for the sake of the herring fishery. The chief produce is oats, barley and black cattle. I was informed that above three thousand are annually sold out of these parts.' The main routes along which these three thousand or more were driven out of Lleyn ran through the lanes a little to the north of Pwllheli. Along these lanes, cattle from the west would have been joined by those from the main cattle markets on the coast. One such meeting place was the village of Rhŷd-y-clafdy

1726

328349

50

If you go east through that village a little way and then follow a public footpath sign on your right, you will find yourself on a clearly marked drove route. In summer this path is very overgrown and the southern half of it has been ploughed up, making it impossible to follow it to its logical conclusion at the village of Penrhos. However, you can take it to the top of a small hill, looking eastwards from which you have a fine view of the green pastures of Lleyn.

Going back to Rhŷd-y-clafdy, you must now follow the lane to Efailnewydd, another place where the cattle would have gathered, and so on to the village of Four Crosses. This ancient settlement has little to offer today. It is an ugly village of unimaginative new housing, and the standing stone which the guide books promise you is in a scrubby paddock behind the Harlech Freezer Factory. From here the road goes east to Llanystumdwy, which has a fine eighteenth-century bridge. The first documentary evidence of a bridge here dates from 1617, but it is likely that there was one before that.

From here the droves went eastwards through Criccieth and Pentrefelin. Opposite the post office in the second village, take a lane to your left which leads to the village of Penmorfa, from where the journey through the main part of North Wales begins.

Robert Jones, the drover, whose Account Book was described by the historian R. T. Jenkins in the *Journal of the Carmarthenshire Historical Society* in 1945, brought sheep through these parts in the early spring. He was taking them to London via Pinner and Edgware. Pigs, making a steady six miles a day, also came through Penmorfa on their way east, driven by Robert Jones and his fellows. Robert Jones's account covers the years from July 8th, 1823 to November 1st, 1837 intermittently, and a couple of verses of hymns occur among the details of the movements of the animals. He died near Criccieth on September 3rd, 1859, and his obituary described him as a saint. He was in any case a man whom his descendants, the Armstrong-Joneses of Tabor, should be proud to claim as an ancestor.

Holiness and learning are Celtic qualities of which the drovers had their fair share. Five of them, including the eighteenth-century Hugh Parry of Penmorfa, joined Dr Johnson, who visited these parts in 1774, in subscribing to the *Wales Golden Treasury*. It is interesting to speculate on whether Hugh Parry would have met the great doctor and whether, as is more likely, he would have gone to listen to Howell Harris, the evangelist and progressive farmer of Brecon, who came to preach in the chapel here in the late eighteenth century.

One thing is certain. Hugh Parry would not recognize his

countryside now. The motor traffic, the railway and the pine trees would probably cause him less astonishment than the new farm lands created by William Maddock's draining of the Traeth Mawr marshes in the 1820s and the building of the town which bears his name, now Welshed into Porthmadog. In Hugh Parry's time the wide estuary of the Glaslyn River extended far inland, and there would have been no possibility of taking the cattle along the westerly part of the road which now runs north-east from Tremadog to Beddgelert. Instead, the droves would have had to travel back a little way in a north-westerly direction. Do not go along the main A487, but take the lane which runs for a little while almost parallel with it, until it turns steeply up hill to the north at Carreg-frêch. From here take the lane to the right, which leads by the Cwmystradllyn River to the foothills of the Dolbenmaen range, a group of hills from which it is said a wave of evil, almost as tangible as the Gulf Stream, runs into these marshy highlands.

Mawddach estuary and Porth-madog

Certainly some violent things have happened here. On the left-hand side of the lane on which you are now walking, and along which geese as well as sheep and cattle were driven to the markets, there is one lonely house, now owned as a holiday cottage by an English doctor. This house, Ty Neuadd, was once owned by two brothers; one was a drover and the other a blacksmith, who worked with a portable forge on this road, which lies between Brynkir in the west and Prenteg in the east. These brothers, both bachelors, were highly thought of in the neighbourhood. The droving brother could always be trusted to bring back all the money that the beasts made in the English sales and distribute it properly to the farmers. It was probably this very esteem in which his brother was held, together with envy for the adventurous life he led, that eventually drove the stay-at-home blacksmith mad. He must have nursed his violent jealousy all the time his brother was making his last trip, for when the drover came back he waylaid him and killed him, ostensibly for the money he carried.

Once past the site of that murder, you will find that the lane branches. Take the right-hand way. It will bring you to a cottage above the small lake of Llyn Du, which is noted for a beautiful spread of water lilies in early spring. Turn right here and walk along the foot of the crags of Mynydd Gorllwyn. This

544426

563428

Llyn Du and standing stones on the Prenteg road

is the haunt of some of the most interesting birds of Merioneth. It also seems to be a gathering place for cuckoos. I've been told that thirteen were once seen by the shores of the lake.

586415   The lane descends steeply to the village of Prenteg, where you turn left for Aber Glaslyn Bridge. But if you have time, and want to challenge the evils of the Dolbenmaen, it is worth making at least two round walks in this area.

Map A page 58   For the first walk, take the path running west from 553441 past Traian Farm and along the slopes of the mountains to join the track at 534442. This joins a farm track, which skirts the north 524437 and west sides of a wood and brings you to the farm of Brynkir. From the farmyard take the track going to the south-east, keeping to the southern edges of the woods. When you reach the last of the trees, take the path that climbs over the hill on your 533424 right. This brings you to Clenenney Farm. When you get on to the lane you will see a telephone box at the junction on your left. The lane going directly south leads you back to Penmorfa, and that on your left is the lane to Prenteg.

The second walk leaves the Prenteg lane at 552421. The path goes over the hills above Tremadog until it reaches the crags of Allt-wen. It keeps above them running to the south-east and then makes a steep descent to the plain. Before it gets to the 563404 main road it joins a farm track. Follow this round to your left and you will come to Shelley's house of Tan-yr allt. Just outside the gates leading to the drive of the house, you will see a public 565405 footpath sign on your left directing you to a grass path which climbs fairly steeply through a field and then enters a little wood. Take the left-hand path when you get into the wood, cross over the stream by the stepping stones, and take the path that climbs through the wood to a gate in the stone wall.

Now follow the track along the ridge to your right. From this point you can see the whole of the drained marshlands. The hillside track disappears after a little while, but if you continue a few hundred yards to the east, you will come to a little bright green meadow, and the house of Pont Ifan with its beautiful stone barn. The lane that leads north from this farm eventually 567413 turns east at the old farm house of Erwsuran to join the lane above Prenteg.

The owner of Pont Ifan lives at Tan-yr allt, where he keeps company with a regular ghost. The phantom is a gentleman in a three-cornered hat and long cloak, and is generally thought to be the spirit of an eighteenth-century farmer of the neighbourhood. If that is so, perhaps Shelley saw him too. And as Tan-yr allt's ghostly visitor is reputed to have a macabre and terrifying sense of humour, it may have accounted for the poet's conviction that he was the victim of an attempted murder. Thomas Love Peacock, Shelley's friend, wrote the episode off as a piece of heightened imagination, but Shelley was convinced that someone had fired a pistol at him. He might have had good reason to be nervous, for he wasn't much liked in the locality. The shepherds in the area were greatly incensed by his habit of killing off the sick sheep he found on his walks without attempting to save them. And his popularity was not enhanced by the fervour with which he welcomed Maddock's plans for draining the marshes – a scheme which put an end to the shipbuilding in the Glaslyn River.

4056 It is worth making a break in your walk to go down the lane from Tan-yr-allt and visit the little town of Tremadog. This is one of the earliest and best examples of town planning. Here Maddock built his 'new town' on the turnpike road to the east. And it was here, in 1888, that Lawrence of Arabia was born.

, 5841 Whether you go east from Tremadog by road, or take the lanes
660409 through the hills, you will have to pass by the village of Prenteg. From here you can either go along the lanes to Tan-y-bwlch, or take the much longer and more interesting way over the mountains. If you are doing part of the journey with a car, however, it might be worth following the road way.

The first part of the trip goes straight across the drained marshes, so it wasn't until the nineteenth century that any drovers could have come this way. From Prenteg you take the short road to Llanfrothen, and when you come into the hamlet
613418 of Garreg you cross the main road and take the lane sign-posted to Rhyd. You are now on a road that was used by the drovers for centuries. At its highest point, where it bends sharply to the
634419 east, the drovers from Lleyn turned round to take one last look at the Caernarvonshire mountains of their home, before turning east to face 'Lladron Meirion' – the wild men of Merioneth.

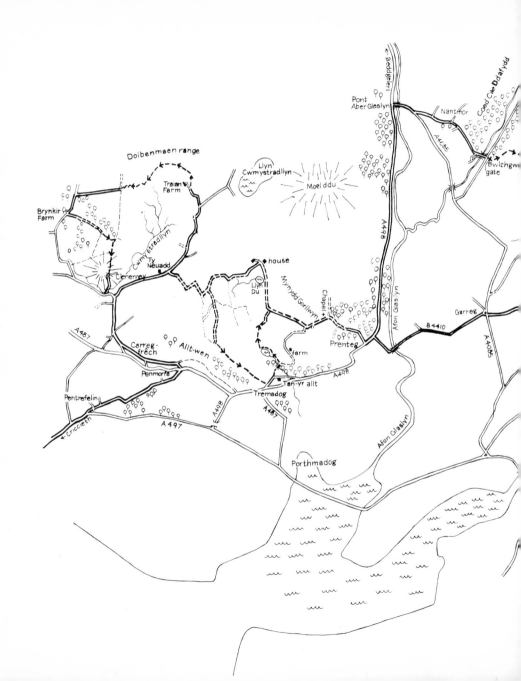

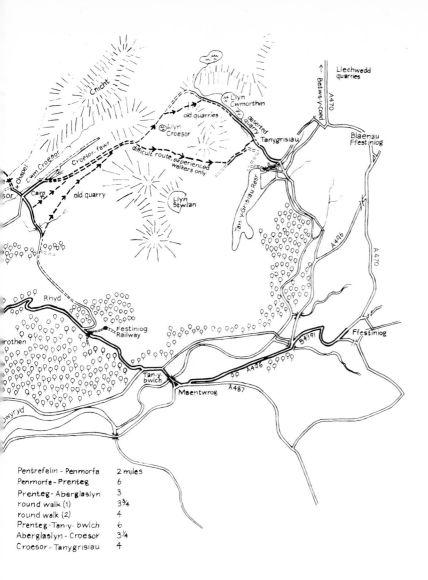

Pentrefelin - Penmorfa   2 miles
Penmorfa - Prenteg   6
Prenteg - Aberglaslyn   3
round walk (1)   3¾
round walk (2)   4
Prenteg - Tan-y-bwlch   6
Aberglaslyn - Croesor   3¼
Croesor - Tanygrisiau   4

The lane takes you through to Tan-y-bwlch, where drovers from three areas converged. It is well known today as one of the main stations for the privately run Festiniog Railway, which makes use of many of the old rail tracks first put down so that the slate from the quarries at Blaenau Ffestiniog could be taken to the ships at Porthmadog. Now the railway is largely used by holiday visitors, and by some local farmers who enjoy its dispensation from the static licensing laws that affect bars. If you take a trip on it you will see much of the country that the drovers covered and which you may not have time to walk. For the actual walks in this area see page 73.

In the eighteenth century, when the Glaslyn River was busy with shipping, the drovers would have had to go north from Prenteg towards Beddgelert, before they could reach Tan-y-bwlch. There has been a bridge across the Glaslyn from this road since the sixteenth century. In 1596 it was listed as one of the five bridges in the county of Merioneth, and at that time ships were brought up to it at high tide. Now the modern, utilitarian road bridge carries streams of cars in the holiday season.

Over the bridge the road runs south to Garreg and Rhyd, and many of the drovers from Lleyn would have followed it. There is a more interesting way though, and one which has always been used in moving sheep in this part of Snowdonia. To reach it, after you have crossed the Glaslyn Bridge, walk a little way south along the main road, and then take the lane on your left, which is sign-posted to Nantmor.

Follow this lane through the village until you cross the bridge at Bwlchgwernog. This is a T junction. The left-hand way takes you through the Cae Ddafydd Forest towards Snowdon; the right-hand way brings you back on the road to Garreg. The path you want starts through a gate at the side of the wood directly opposite you.

Paved road, Croesor

612452

This is the old road that runs to the village of Croesor, and which is still paved in places with stones that were probably placed there before the Romans came to Wales. This track is easy to follow. Just before you reach Croesor village a sign on your left directs you to the Cnicht Mountain, a simple

645466

afternoon's climb on a clear day and well worth the diversion from your main route. Yet, like all mountains, it needs to be treated with respect. In low cloud or high winds the narrow paths on the ledges leading up the summit can be dangerous for the ill-prepared.

The old road brings you into Croesor village past the chapel and the post office. The post office is now simply that. Croesor has no shop, but at one time the village store here was run by

Old Croesor road

Showell Styles, the writer, mountaineer and great authority on the walks of Wales. He now lives in Porthmadog.

632446

6845

When you get to the cross-roads in Croesor, you will find that the right-hand lane takes you down to the hamlet of Llanfrothen; ignore this way if you are setting out to walk over the mountains to Tanygrisiau. The way to your left, or the lane ahead of you sign-posted to Tan-y-bwlch, will both serve, but it is probably more interesting to start off along the lane on your left.

Above Slate wall, Croesor

Croesor area

640452   This will bring you to a row of cottages where the lane ends. The track goes on to the right to climb the mountainside by the disused slate quarries. Still climbing, take the path to the left.

662457   This goes to the north of Llyn Croesor, passes more ruined quarries and eventually turns south to run by the westerly

678460   shores of the steel grey mountain waters of Llyn Cwmorthin. At the southern end of the lake, a little wooden footbridge brings you to a desolation of old slate workings above Tanygrisiau, and the steep descent into that village.

The better-made, right-hand lane from the Croesor quarries takes you to Tanygrisiau by a shorter, but equally dramatic

666454   route. It climbs steeply to the craggy pass above the new reservoir, and comes out on to the road that runs between the dam and Tanygrisiau village. This is quite a difficult route and

only experienced hill-walkers should attempt it.

Should you take the Tan-y-bwlch road from Croesor, you can choose between two tracks running off the road on your left, climbing the mountains that lie between it and Tanygrisiau. 634443 The first leaves the road by the first small stream you come to as you walk eastwards. It is virtually a sheep run through the bracken, but rudimentary cairns direct you to the ridge of Croesor-fawr, where you join the track above the slate quarry below Llyn Croesor. The rest of the way follows the route given above. You can also reach this track by continuing along the 635438 Tan-y-bwlch road until you cross a second stream. In that case the path you take runs along the eastern slopes of the fawr, and meets the main track at 650454. From here you can take a path running north-west of Llyn Croesor, once you are past the quarries at 657456.

From Tanygrisiau you can either go back and take up the story from Tan-y-bwlch, or carry on east to Ysbyty Ifan. I'll take the second alternative first.

It means walking along the road to the slate-quarrying town of Blaenau Ffestiniog. If you can so organize your day that you can take at least a couple of hours in this town, it is well worth turning your attention from the drovers to the quarry workers. If you go half a mile (804 metres) along the A470, which leaves

Left Slate quarry above Croesor
Right Disused slate quarries at Tanygrisiau

the town by the railway station at the end of the High Street, you will find a sign on your right directing you to the Llechwedd Slate Caverns. Here, a reconstruction of nineteenth-century quarrying has been arranged in the surface sheds, and in the depths of the mountain. Some of the twenty-five miles (forty kilometres) of underground workings have been fitted with a railway track so that visitors can see the quarrying sites.

From the caverns, you can take a bus running north-east

Left Llyn Cwmorthin and Tanygrisiau
Right Quarry above Croesor

723524

towards Betws-y-Coed. The road, which partly follows the
medieval highway from Conwy to Ardudwy, passes the dramatic castle ruin of Dolwyddelan. Legend has it that Llewellyn the
Great was born here. The gaunt, square keep that guards this
valley dates from the thirteenth century. Throughout the
centuries there was a fortification here, so that the English lords
could control the route from the mountains to the west coast.

7352

The village lies a mile (1.6 kilometres) further along the road.
Leave the bus here, and follow the route that the twin drovers,
Moses and Aaron Jones, took to the south-east. Opposite the
bus stop you will find a road bridge crossing the Afon Lledr,
sign-posted to the railway station. Once over the bridge you will
see a wide track running north-east between the river and the

Above Castle ruin, Dolwyddelan
Right Between Penmachno and
Ysbyty Ifan

746525   edge of the forest land. Go along it until you come to a path on your right. This path climbs steeply through the forest and comes out on the mountainside, where it runs due east to the next stretch of forest land. Follow the track through the forest

770526   until it joins a lane, then turn right.

7950   This lane brings you to the village of Penmachno. Go straight through the village over the Afon Machno, and take the small road which runs to your right by the Machno Arms. It is marked with a 'No Through Road' sign, and goes due south. When it ends at the junction of two farm tracks, take the one on the left, which goes through a gate, past an old car dump. After that unpromising start it runs through sedges on to the hills. This is an ancient road, paved in places, and where it has been fenced across good wooden steps are provided for walkers. It runs across a valley, and crosses the Rhydyrhalen and Eidda rivers. It then climbs on to the hills above the Ysbyty Ifan road. Here it becomes a farm track going through a gated road leading

836484   to the farm of Hafod Ifan, about a quarter of a mile (402 metres) to the south of the village.

678421   To go to Tan-y-bwlch from Tanygrisiau (see map A), you can either walk down the footpath to the south of the dam, and then take a short trip by the Festiniog Railway from Dduallt station, or you can make the journey by road along the vale of Ffestiniog to Maentwrog. If you decide on that course, you will have a more pleasant walk if you take the minor road which runs to the north of the river. You reach it by leaving the A470

687416   at Pont Tal-y-bont.

You must thank a stalwart old lady for the beautiful deciduous forests above Tan-y-bwlch. When she sold her land to the Forestry Commission, she firmly inserted a clause to the effect that no conifers were to be planted there. This means that the north side of the estuary is much as the drovers would have known it.

Tan-y-bwlch was an important centre for the drovers of North Wales and many of them had their homes in this area. Among

Left and below Ysbyty Ifan road

them was William Rowland, who kept an inn in the village. He was so much a part of the establishment of the county of Merioneth that, in 1762, the Michaelmas quarter sessions were adjourned from Dolgellau and held in Rowland's house on Monday, October 25th. The same thing happened at the Easter sessions two years later, when two of the local justices – David Morris, rector of Ffestiniog cum Maentwrog, and Hugh Anwyl, landowner of Trawsfynydd, Llandecwyn and Gwyddehoern – were in attendance. William Rowland was described as a 'top-

Near Trawsfynydd

man drover', which means that he would also have been a dealer.

Another great drover of the time, and no doubt a relation, was Rowland Edmund, who also farmed at Felinrhyd-fawr, which lies across the river from Tan-y-bwlch. He died in 1819 and is buried in the crowded little chapel cemetery that stands on the hill above Harlech Castle. His history has been recorded in the *Merioneth Journal* by Dr Lewis Lloyd of Coleg Harlech.[2] Dr Lloyd discovered Edmund's will, which shows that he left £963 and died owning cows to the value of £80, steers to £30, sheep to £150, pigs to £3 and horses to £30. This all added up to a sizeable fortune for those days. Edmund had two sons, both of whom were farmer-drovers. The elder became a tenant at Llandecwyn, according to the sensible Welsh practice which did not expect the eldest son to wait for his father's death before he branched out on his own. The younger, Edward, eventually took over the family farm.

The herds that collected at Tan-y-bwlch travelled south-east to Maentwrog, and then north-east to Ffestiniog. There they would have been joined by the cattle from the Llandecwyn area north of Harlech, and by those herds from Trawsfynydd that were not being driven east to Bala.

Map B page 75 If you want to take a look at this part of the country, go round the head of the estuary from Tan-y-bwlch to Maentwrog. From that village follow the road towards Harlech for a couple of miles. Leave it when you come to a track on your left, about a 644396 mile (1.6 kilometres) past the power station. This forest path will bring you out to the reservoir of Llyn Tecwyn-uchaf. Keep to its north-westerly shore until you come to the track leading 633376 to the village of Llandecwyn.

From here, go south until you come to a lane going round the northern shore of a small lake. Turn left and follow the bends of the lane, ignoring the first turn off it to your left (unless you are going to follow the second walk in this area) and the next to your right. The way you want climbs to the farm of Caerwych. There the lane ends and a farm track takes you on to the east 653364 and the lonely farmstead of Nant-Pasgan-bâch. In Harlech they still tell the story of the drover who was killed on these heights for the sake of the money he was bringing back.

At Nant-Pasgan-bâch leave the track for the footpath on your right. This takes you across the crags to the east, and through desolate mountain country until you come to the lane that runs 684358 along the western shores of Trawsfynydd lake.

668387 A shorter and less hazardous walk, which avoids the crags above Cwm Moch, takes you past a splendid waterfall. To reach it you must double back on your tracks, taking the lane on your left as you leave the lake beyond Llandecwyn. Follow the lane to a 658378 small lake, Llyn Llennyrch. When the track divides, take the left-hand path which runs under pylon wires into the forest. The winding descent through these trees takes you to the waterfall. Now turn right and follow the course of the stream to 674376 the dams at the head of Trawsfynydd lake. Turn right along the track which runs along the western shores of the lake and by the plantation of Coed y Rhygen, until you come out on to the lane which you would have reached if you had taken the mountain path.

Follow this lane by the lake until you meet the main road (A470 Porthmadog – Dolgellau) at Cefn-gallt-y-cwm. Turn left here and go past Trawsfynydd to Pont Islyn, where you will find a track running due east. The eerie wailing you may begin to hear

708372

Near Trawsfynydd

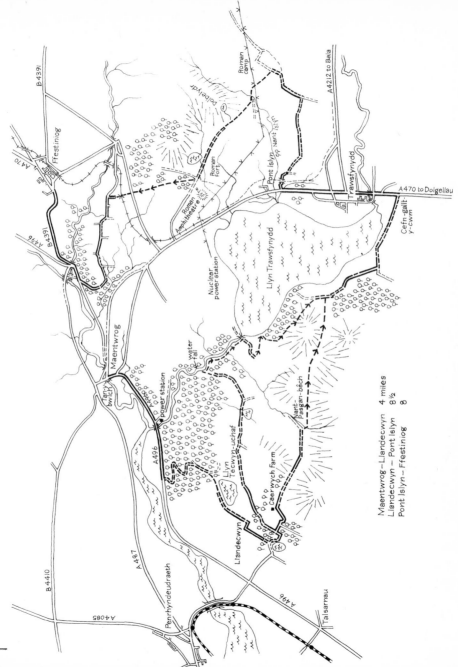

Map B

after you have walked a little way will probably be familiar by now; it comes from the high pylons to the north. On a dull day it adds to the strange bleakness of this part of the country. No wonder that in this stretch of land, which still bears traces of the legions who were stationed here, many weird stories have come out of the mists of people who have seen the ghostly soldiers marching across the hills.

Roman fort near Trawsfynydd

When the track divides take the left-hand path, which will brin

you to the remains of a Roman camp (Hadrian's Wall must have been a pleasant posting after this) and the marshy lands of Nant Islyn. Here you cross beneath the pylon wires, keeping the hill of Dolbelydr to your right. The track along the side of the hill brings you to the disused slate workings of Nant Twll. From here, if you turn to the west you will see one of the clearest examples of how man's technology has left its mark on the landscape over the centuries. The slate quarry lies to your left, in the distance is the nuclear power station of Trawsfynydd,

and just ahead of you is the steep little mound of a Roman fort, with an amphitheatre to the north of it. Keep along the track running west towards it, and when that track becomes a lane take a path through the forest on your right. This comes out on to a stretch of open hill, and runs almost due north for the main road to Ffestiniog. Cross that road and take the footpath, which crosses a disused railway line and then joins a lane. Turn left here and follow the curve of the path for some three miles (4.8 kilometres) to Ffestiniog village.

707389

704408

You may decide to follow the drove routes from Ffestiniog by car, at least to the point where the drove ways cross the A5. If you are going to do that take the road to Bala, and where the road divides at Pont yr Afon-Gam take the left-hand fork for Ysbyty Ifan. However, if you have time for a short excursion, it's worthwhile following the right-hand road for some way first. This minor road to Bala was used by drovers on their way to England, and on the return journey, although through the years several slight alterations have been made to its course. Just before it meets the new A road, built when the railway line was drowned by the flooding of Llyn Celyn to form a reservoir, it crosses a stream. At this point you will notice, a little way to the north, the old bridge which the road once went over.

746419

The story, as I had it from Captain Sandy Livingstone – Learmonth of Tan-yr allt, is that a Dolgellau drover was once forced to hide beneath the old bridge. He was returning home with the money he had made from his deals when he discovered, just to the east of Bala, that he was being followed into the town by an unknown man, on a very powerful horse. To throw the pursuer off his track he stopped at the White Lion, and in a roundabout way asked help of the landlord.

The drover requested that he should be treated in such a way that everyone at the inn would think he was staying the night. However, he made it clear that this was not the case, and that on no account was his pony to be given much to eat. The drover then described his pursuer and requested that when he arrived at the inn the landlord was to be sure to give him an extra large dinner and to see to it that his horse had double rations. This was done, and no sooner had the stranger settled down to eat, than the drover set off smartly to the west.

When he had gone about half-way to Ffestiniog he realized that the time he had bought himself with his trick had come to an end, for hooves were thundering along the road behind him. So he leapt off his pony and dragged it under the bridge. When he heard his pursuer galloping overhead, he gave him time to get well out of earshot and then set out south through the mountains to Trawsfynydd. There he alerted the officers of the law, who were in time, so the story goes, to arrest the confused would-be robber at Ffestiniog.

763437 Your main route runs from Pont yr Afon-Gam north-east across the wide marshlands and peat bogs to Ysbyty Ifan. The present minor road was a track in droving times, and you must keep with it, for the impassable peat bog comes right up to the side of the road. After some two miles (3.2 kilometres) you will find that the road divides. The left-hand fork takes you to the village of Penmachno Cwm, once a busy slate-quarrying area, now almost entirely a holiday village. At this fork there is a large well, providing water for men and beasts. It has stood there for many centuries, but the present stone buildings that surround it were put up in 1846. The inscription reads *Ffynnon eidda yf a bydd ddiolchgar*, 'Drink and be thankful'. Beside the well is the remaining wall of a large compound where pigs were gathered for the journey to the east. Carry on along the road to Ysbyty Ifan, and from there to Pentrefoelas on the A5.

8751 Pentrefoelas was a gathering place for the cattle, who would then have gone east through Rhyd-lydan and Glasfryn to the shoeing station of Cerrigydrudion. It was at Pentrefoelas that the eighteenth-century drovers might have met the youthful Twm o'r Nant, who died in 1810. They might even have provided him with the theme of his satires, which often savagely attacked the knavery and bad habits of the cattle men.

Twm o'r Nant's real name was Thomas Edwards, and a portrait of him at the age of seventy-one is inscribed 'The Cambrian Shakespeare'. Without a knowledge of Welsh it is difficult to decide how apt that title is, for no complete translations of his dramatic interludes have been published. The nearest you can get to them is Dedwydd Jones's play *Bard*. It deals with the life and times of Twm o'r Nant and incorporates some of his work. This play was commissioned by the Sherman Theatre, University College, Cardiff and was published in 1974 by the Cokaygne Press in Cambridge.

Twm o'r Nant once kept a toll gate in South Wales, but he left the job after two years because he couldn't stand the hauntings. George Borrow was told that what troubled him were 'ghosts and goblins and unearthly things, particularly phantom hearses, which used to pass through the gates at midnight, without paying, when the gate was shut.' Twm first came to Pentrefoelas before his toll-keeping days when, having got into a fight in the north, he had to flee south across the Hiraethog Mountains. He was about twenty-three at the time, and he later reported that it was then that he became acquainted 'with another of the same propensity for collecting old books, viz. an old man at Pentrefoelas, who read in the chapel on Sunday and made clogs at other times'. The holy clogmaker was Sion Dafydd, who died in 1769 at the age of ninety-four, and is buried in Ysbyty Ifan churchyard.

Pentrefoelas is most worth visiting today for its mill and bakery. It is difficult to imagine that in the 1920s and '30s the A5, on which the town lies, was a narrow, muddy road. Now it has a pavement, to keep the walker out of the way of the continual flow of heavy traffic, but you won't want to follow it all the way east to Cerrigydrudion. There are two ways of avoiding its present horrors.

If you are going to keep to the north of the main road, take the footpath that is sign-posted beside Pentrefoelas church. This brings you out on the road to Denbigh. Turn left along it for a 879519 little way and then take the first farm track on your right. 893518 When this meets the lane turn right again towards the A5. Here you must walk along the A5 until you come to the village of Glasfryn, where you turn left and follow the lane which will bring you out on the Ruthin road above Cerrigydrudion.

In dry weather it is possible to avoid a section of A5 walking by 893519 turning north when the lane divides and going past the farm of Gors-Nûg. When this lane comes to a T junction turn right and 933505 follow the lanes and footpaths that run south-east to Cefn-brîth. This is about five miles (eight kilometres). This way should not be attempted whenever there has been prolonged rain as the footpath crosses marsh ground to the north of the small lake of Llyn y Cwrt.

The other possibility is to go south of the A5, crossing the bridge that lies immediately opposite the Voelas Arms. Follow the lane round to the left and either join the A5 just beyond Rhyd-lydan or go south for a couple of miles and then take the left-hand turn for Pant-y-griafolen and Glasfryn, where you have to join the A5. The most famous drover from the shoeing station of Cerrigydrudion was Edward Morus. He is better remembered as a poet than as a drover, though his achievements in both occupations were remarkable. He was still droving at the age of eighty-two, and he died in Essex in 1689. His brother Huw Morus, also a bard, composed a metrical lament to mark his death. You follow Edward's route by going north out of the village along the Denbigh road, and leaving it almost immediately for the B5105 to Ruthin.

893498

Map C page 82

961486
Leave this road by the first lane on your right, and follow it up the hill to the farm of Tŷ-mawr. At this point you will see a causeway track on your right which crosses a patch of swampy land. This brings you through three fields to a path, much overgrown with heather in many places, which runs east round the slopes of Mwdwl-eithin. Follow this path until you come to a stile over a wire fence. A stone wall runs round the side of the hill at this point, and if you keep it on your right, you will eventually come to a place where the lane divides three ways. Take the central path, which will bring you to the farm of Rhos-caer-ceiliog at the bend of a lane. The lane ahead will bring you to a track running due east over a hill to the village of Tycerrig. Turn right here, and then at the cross-roads go left towards Bettws Gwerfil Goch. At that village turn right, and then take the first road on the left which climbs steeply to come out on a lane, whose unusually wide verges signify that this was once a drove way. This lane comes out on the main Ruthin to Bala road, just south of the village of Gwyddelwern.

023461
0346
033464

075464

From that village take the steep lane on your right just opposite the church, and follow it for about a mile (1.6 kilometres). At the second corner in a double bend of the lane, you will notice a track on your left. It runs between two steep banks and is very overgrown in places; so much so in fact that at some points you

087462

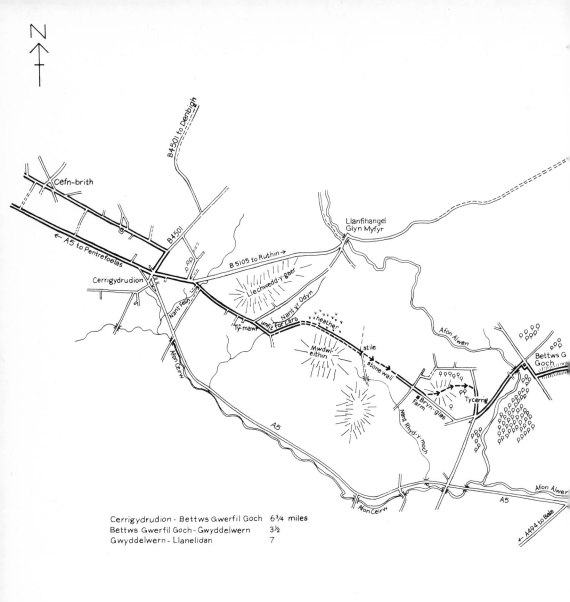

N

B4501 to Denbigh

Cefn-brith

A5 to Pentrefoelas

B4501

Cerrigydrudion

B5105 to Ruthin →

Llechwedd-y-gaer

Llanfihangel
Glyn Myfyr

Nant Felin

Nant yr Odyn

Tŷ-mawr

unfit for cars

heather

stile

Afon Alwen

Bettws G
Goch

Mwdwl
eithin

stone wall

Afon Ceirw

A5

Bryn-glas
Farm

Nant Rhyd-y-moch

Tycerrig

Afon Ceirw

A5

Afon Alwen

A494 to Bala

Cerrigydrudion - Bettws Gwerfil Goch   6¾ miles
Bettws Gwerfil Goch - Gwyddelwern   3½
Gwyddelwern - Llanelidan   7

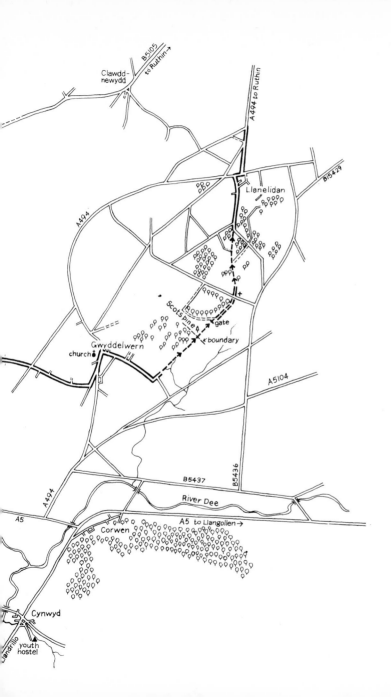

Map C

will have to climb over the fence on your left and walk along the field beside the track.

Unfortunately, when you get to the stream that marks the old county boundary you will find the track has been wired across. If you risk a trespass by climbing through this, you will find the track even more clearly marked. It runs past a straggle of larches and one Scots pine, which was probably planted as a way mark. It gets slightly fainter as it goes through a field, but

the track is still clear enough, and you make your way on to a lane through a small wooden, wicket gate. Follow this to the right until you reach a lane; opposite you is a corrugated-iron chapel. Turn left along this lane and then almost immediately right along a farm track, which will bring you to a path running due north until it comes out on a lane about a mile (1.6 kilometres) to the south of the village of Llanelidan.

103480

105494

From Llanelidan take the lane which goes north to meet the main road for Ruthin. This town makes a good centre for the rest of the walks in this section. George Borrow found Ruthin a dull town, although he liked to dwell on its history; standing on an eminence in the Clwyd valley, it has naturally been the centre of every skirmish from the Iron Age raids to the battles of the Civil War. For our purpose the Ruthin fairs are more interesting than its fights. The Council Book of Ruthin for 1642 to 1695 records how and when these were held during the seventeenth century. This is how Norman Tucker transcribed the entry for 1646 for the *Denbighshire Historical Society Journal* of 1960:

Be it remembered that Ruthin Fayre is always to be kept ye 28th day of July and the 29th except it falls to be on a Sunday . . . This fayre was kept before some fourscore yeares agone as is remembered by some alive this present and our charters do mencon yt neare upon 400 yeares agow the warres and troubles forced us to forgett ourselves. There were likewise beastes to be sould every munday and corne markett every mundays and Frydayes which customs wee hope the town will encourage and keep up as formerly wch will be for all peoples forever.

The Ruthin fairs were a meeting place for the drovers, who came into the town from the north and the west. There was a Drovers' Arms at Rhewl Buarthau, a little to the north of the town, lying on the Denbighshire road. The Denbighshire drovers who came this way were very important people. In 1636 they were entrusted with carrying the ship tax money to London, a levy which the Welsh landowners with their miles of coastline were content to settle. A few miles to the south-east is the village of Graig-fechan, where the Three Pigeons was enlarged in the eighteenth century in order to accommodate the increasing numbers of drovers heading for Wrexham and Shrewsbury.

Near Cerrigydrudion

Map D page 87 To start on that way from Ruthin, you must first make for the road junction to the east of the town, and then take the minor road which runs between the main roads for Mold and Wrexham. When that road divides take the right-hand way and follow it to the B5429. Turn right here until you reach a point 144567 where three lanes lead up into the hills on your left. The central one of these is marked 'No Through Road'. Follow it up a hill, past some farm buildings and along the side of a little wood running east. At the corner of a field you will see another track running down the hill to your right. If you follow that it will bring you back to a lane. Turn right by the telephone box, and you will find you are about a mile (1.6 kilometres) from the place where you left the B road.

If you are not going to make that circular trip, you will find the way to the east by climbing to your left. When you reach the ridge of the hills another possibility for a circular walk is 168558 offered. Offa's Dyke crosses the ridge at this point, and if you follow it for a couple of miles to the south past a piece of forest 172543 land and across a lane, you will find immediately on your right a track running directly to the west. This brings you out at Graig-fechan and the Three Pigeons.

The old cattle ways, of course, went due east. The northerly track, which you are on if you didn't deviate along Offa's Dyke, brings you out on to the lane that leads to the village of 190563 Llanarmon-yn-Ial. This was an important droving village and at one time boasted ten inns. Twenty-one years ago the present landlord of the Raven Inn (the one remaining pub) installed petrol pumps by his garage and discovered many ox cues. If you have time to wander a little round the countryside of this village, which was enclosed in 1830, you will find that it is a potted history of Welsh quarrying. The lead mines gradually petered out, one after another, at the end of last century but the stone quarries, after a temporary decline, are again flourishing and expanding – and making life miserable for all who live near them.

The village must have been quite prosperous in the nineteenth century, for besides the quarrying it was one of the few places in Wales where wheat was grown. To make that possible, and to provide the good grazing that the drovers from Ruthin would

86

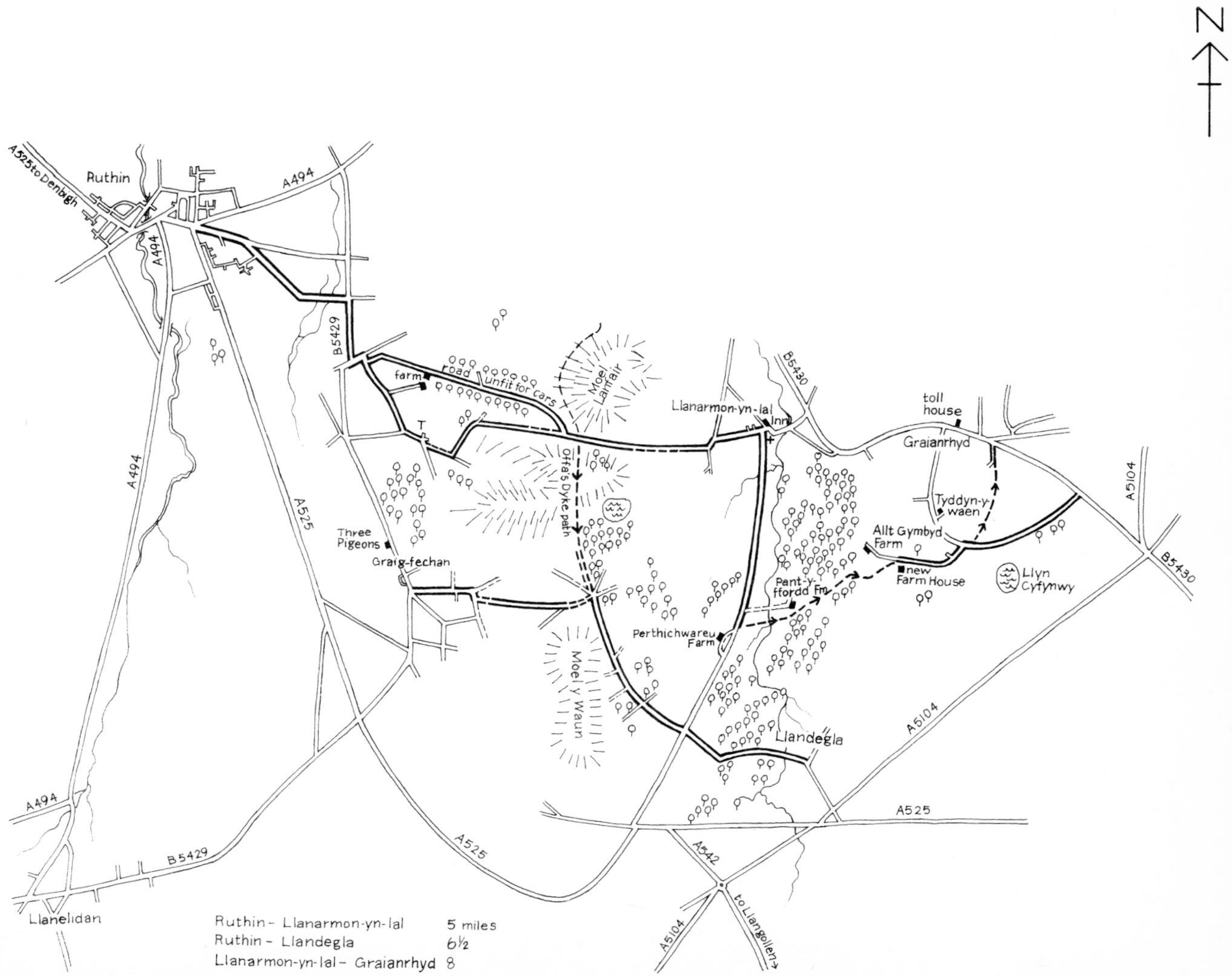

Map D

N

toll house

Graianrhyd

A5104

B5430

Llyn Cyfynwy

Tydyn-y-waen

Allt Gymbyd Farm

new Farm House

Pant-y-ffordd fm

Llandegla

A5104

A525

A542

to Llangollen →

A5104

Llanarmon-yn-ial

B5430

Perthichwareu Farm

Moel Lanfair

Offa's Dyke path

Moel y Waun

A525

road unfit for cars

farm

Three Pigeons

Graig-fechan

B5429

A494

A525

A494

B5429

Ruthin

A494

A525 to Denbigh

Llanelidan

A494

Ruthin – Llanarmon-yn-ial   5 miles
Ruthin – Llandegla   6½
Llanarmon-yn-ial – Graianrhyd   8

have appreciated, the land was regularly treated with lime. This was slowly burnt before being crushed and spread on the ground, and every farm in the area had its own stone, beehive-shaped lime kiln. You can see one of these on the lane

198576

to the neighbouring village of Eryrys. The kiln stands in a little wood on the left of the road.

From Llanarmon-yn-Ial the droves were taken south to Llan-

190562

degla. To get there take the B road to the west of Llanarmon church, and follow it until you come to the ancient farm house of Perthichwareu to your right. At that point you will find on

189540

your left a grass track running between two steep banks. This leads to a gate into a field. Cross it diagonally to your right towards the farm of Pant-y-ffordd. Behind the farm buildings the path climbs the hill and goes through some woods to emerge in a field at the ridge of a hill. Here you can see traces of a fairly wide track. Follow it round to your right till you come to a wicket gate, which brings you out into a lane by a new house. Follow this lane to your left until you come to the farm of Allt

205549

Gymbyd. At one time this farm and the surrounding land were the property of the Abbey of Valle Crucis, where ruins stand to the north of Llangollen, and this area is still locally known as the Happy Lands – a popular mutation of Abbey Lands. The path that you have just followed from Perthichwareu is largely

Offa's Dyke

remembered as the way along which the cheeses from the rich

Lime kiln

farms of Llanarmon were taken to the markets.

215551

The track from Allt Gymbyd makes a T junction with a lane. You can either turn right here and follow the lane to the B5430 about a mile (1.6 kilometres) to the north of the main Ruthin to Chester road, or you can take the footpath directly opposite which will bring you to the little village of Graianrhyd about a mile further to the north on that B road. Whichever way the droves took from Allt Gymbyd, they would thus manage to avoid the toll gate which stood across the road to the west of Graianrhyd.

Most of the beasts from these parts would have been taken to Wrexham rather than Chester, and if you want to follow that

249532

path continue south-east with the B5430 until it joins the A525. Here you turn left through the town of Bwlchgwyn, which was another major shoeing station, and so to Wrexham.

Dolgellau

(Ordnance Survey sheet 124)

Llandanwg church

'I always walk in Wales,' said George Borrow, as his wife and step-daughter followed him round by train. It was and is a proper sentiment, even though time does not always make it practicable. However, it is possible to compromise – to take the train towards Harlech, and then walk back with the ghosts of the drovers and the busy trafficking of past centuries across the now empty hills to England. Alternatively, you can make your centre at Dolgellau or Trawsfynydd, and spend your days walking the drove routes and ancient tracks which cover the whole of Ardudwy and the desolate land to the west of Bala. The area extends from the slate quarries in the north to the heavily conifered plantations to the south. Between them lie dramatic folds of ancient rocks, peat bogs and grouse moors.

570286   If you go by train to Harlech, get out at Llandanwg. This little seaside village, whose holiday bungalows stretch through the sands to Harlech, is the start of your journey. Make your way first of all to the tiny church, half-buried in the sand, whose slate grave stones carry inscriptions in Welsh and English dating back to the seventeenth century. Here you will find memorials to the Roberts family, and a John Roberts was one of the last recorded drovers from these parts. Dr Lewis Lloyd of Coleg Harlech has traced his marriage to Mary Griffith, of that parish. It took place in April 1790, and they had eight children; the eldest, Robin or Robert, was born in 1791. He seems to have followed his father's trade. The second son landed up in the workhouse at Penrhyndeudraeth. Another became a seaman at Porthmadog. The fourth, Micah, was the Harlech shoemaker.[3] The church in which this family was christened, married and buried is completely cut off from the world for 364 days of the year. The sand is half-way up the west door, and the windows are heavily barricaded against both sand and holiday litter. But you can just peer inside, and it is quite a shock to see that the pews are all in good order and that candles stand on the altar. The explanation is that once a year a small congregation dig their way into the church and hold a service there.

Beside the church is a large modern car park. On the skyline to the south-east the mountains form a long ridge. The clear notc in that ridge is the Bwlch y Rhiwgyr – the pass of the drovers – through which the sheep and cattle from this coast had to pass on the first stage of their journey to England. The herds from Llandanwg would be joined by cattle driven by the Pughs of Llanfair, a village a little to the south of Harlech. For generations the Pughs drove cattle from these parts. Both the son and the grandson of the Reverend William Pugh, who was rector of Llanfair's Church of St Mary from 1816-45, were drovers, and they went on driving cattle even after the coming of the railways. The grandson, Maurice Pugh, died in 1915. Possibly they would all have collected at Sarn Hir, the road that runs south from Llanfair and which the Llandanwg herds would have had to cross.

From this starting point by the coast, the herds were taken

inland, heading for Bron-y-foel and Cwm Nantcol. From there they went along the old tracks to Bontddu on the Mawddach estuary just west of Dolgellau. From the village of Llanbedr to the south of Sarn Hir, two choices lie before you.

607248

You can either follow the Pughs and the Roberts on the way they must have taken from Bron-y-foel, or you can go right into Cwm Nantcol.

Map E page 94

If you choose the first alternative, you must go along the main road to Dyffryn Ardudwy. There you will see a lane sign-posted for Cwm Nantcol. If you go a little further into the village,

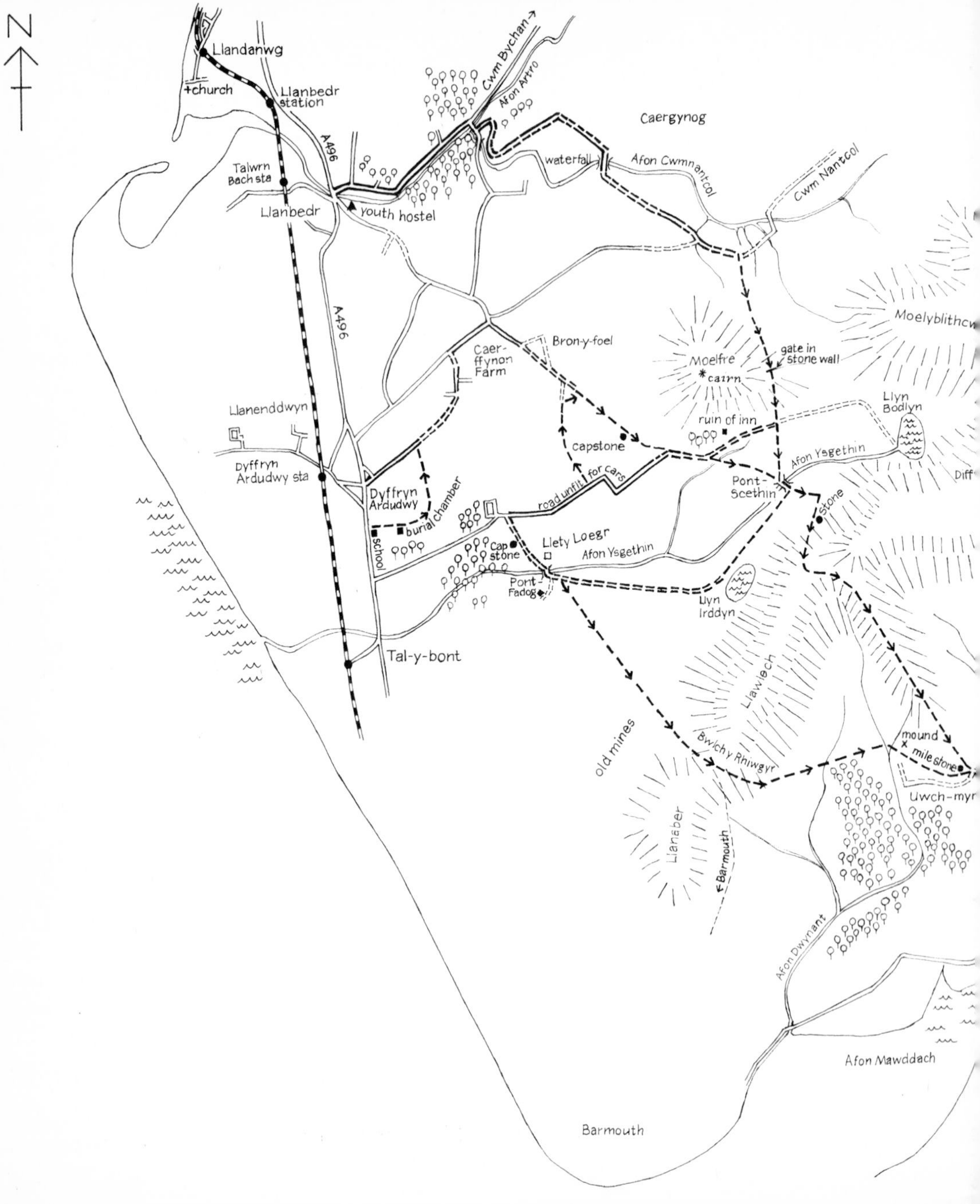
N
Llandanwg
+church
Llanbedr station
Cwm Bychan
Afon Artro
Caergynog
waterfall
Afon Cwmnantcol
Cwm Nantcol
Talwrn Bach sta
A496
Llanbedr
youth hostel
Moelyblithcw
Bron-y-foel
Caer-ffynon Farm
Moelfre
cairn
gate in stone wall
Llyn Bodlyn
Llanenddwyn
ruin of inn
capstone
Afon Ysgethin
Dyffryn Ardudwy sta
road unfit for cars
Pont-Scethin
Dyffryn Ardudwy
burial chamber
stone
school
Cap stone
Llety Loegr
Afon Ysgethin
Pont-Fadog
Llyn Irddyn
Tal-y-bont
Llawlech
old mines
Bwlch y Rhiwgyr
mound
mile stone
Uwch-myr
Llanaber
Barmouth
Afon Dwynant
Afon Mawddach
Barmouth

Llandanwg - Dyffryn Ardudwy	3½ miles
Dyffryn Ardudwy - Bron-y-foel	2¼
Llanbedr - Cwm Nantcol	4¼
Cwm Nantcol - Pont-Scethin	1½
Pont-Scethin - Bontddu	4½
Pont-Scethin - Pont-Fadog	2¾
round walk from Pont-Scethin	6
Pont-Fadog - Bontddu	6
Pont-Fadog - Dolgellau	10½

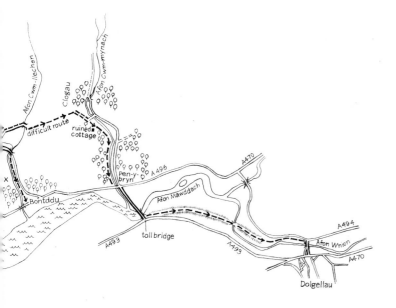

however, you will see another sign, also on your left, directing you to an ancient burial chamber. This path runs beside the school and the prehistoric burial chamber towards a little wood. It is a pretty and popular path. You want the less-frequented and therefore fainter one which climbs due north, crosses a farm track and comes out on the lane a couple of miles below Caer-ffynnon Farm. Turn right and climb up towards the farm; when you reach a little cross-roads turn right through a gate, where the lane soon becomes a grass track.

603249

Aeons before the drovers made their way east, this track was used by Stone Age people slowly venturing eastwards from Ireland in the third millennium B.C. Some of these people stayed and farmed the hillsides around Moelfre, where they built stone huts and a cairn, partly as a religious rite no doubt, but more practically as a way mark. They were buried in the barrow in the plains. Others went further south and east before they died, always looking for richer farming lands. Some of them settled in the lands now drowned by the waters of Cardigan Bay. Their history gave birth to the earliest legends of the Britons which are found in the *Mabinogion*, the Welsh folk tales collected and written down in medieval times. All of them were part of a great west/east migration, which drove men across the shallow seas from Ireland. The memory of the time when it was possible to wade almost all the way from Ireland to mid-Wales is kept alive in the Welsh name for hut circles, *cyttiau gwyddelod* – Irishmen's huts.

Burial chamber at Dyffryn

607247 Moelfre is a strange mountain. From Bron-y-foel the path goes past its gently rounded southern slopes; but should you follow the Cwm Nantcol way, you will find that its craggy northern aspect is forbidding even in bright sunshine.

You can reach Cwm Nantcol by taking the sign-posted gated road from Bron-y-foel. If you do so, you will see some of the very best examples of dry stone walling. The walls are topped with stones, carefully chosen, to make a neat herring-bone pattern. You can also reach Cwm Nantcol from Llanbedr along the sign-posted lane past the Youth Hostel. This lane is very prettily wooded and has a mapped-out nature trail and arrow-marked pathway to a waterfall on your right. At the bridge the road forks, the way to the left going towards the strange and beautiful lake of Cwm Bychan and the 'Roman steps' leading to the rocky heights of Craig Ddrwg. The walks in that direction are outlined on page 115.

600274

The drovers from Llanbedr would have taken the right-hand lane to the south. It soon runs clear of the trees, turns a little to the north-east to avoid the marshes, then goes south again along the slopes of Caergynog to the bridge across the Afon Cwmnantcol. Here you come into the valley, which runs due east to where it appears to be completely shut in by the Rhinog

616268

Mountains. I am continually astonished how each valley south of the Harlech dome has such a markedly individual character. In this one there is an almost eerie contrast between the formidable ancient crags and the luxuriant pastures lying beneath them.

The road running through the western part of the valley is tarmacked now for the sake of the farms, and to make it possible to get the children to school. This part of the lane once had much greater importance, for it was the old London to Harlech road. To follow that old road on its way south, as the drovers would have done, leave the motorable lane at the public footpath sign. The old carriageway is still quite clear, but in many places it has become a watercourse and in the very marshy ground you will have to walk round it. Yet, on the whole, you will find that the old causeways still serve.

It is about forty minutes' climb to the top of the pass between the mountains of Moelfre and Moelyblithcwm, but long before that you will lose sight of the lane winding through the valley and of the farms it serves. Then it is not hard to imagine how robbers and bandits hid in these hills waiting for the London coach, or perhaps for a drover returning westwards with the cash from the sales he had made.

The shadow of the old road winds up the pass, but for stretches you will find that you lose it altogether. It twists to avoid outcrops of rock, and then leads you through stone walls. The last gap in the walls is now gated. At this point the Cwm Nantcol drovers, on the start of their long journey into England, had climbed high enough to be able to take a last look at their home valley, before descending into the Ysgethin valley with its two lakes.

The southern valley is marshy and inhabited only by sheep. The strange thing is that although its surrounding hills are much more rounded than those of Cwm Nantcol, even in bright sunshine it is the bleaker of the two valleys. On its descent into this valley the old road passes the ruins of a coaching inn, once the site of many bandit raids. The most notable of these occurred when a party of fashionable London people stopped there on the way to a large Harlech wedding. The raid is still

630257

talked about in the district.

634241

Just past the remains of the ruined inn, your way will be crossed by another track, running east to Llyn Bodlyn and west to a paved causeway leading to Bron-y-foel. If you go a little way along the path to the west, leaving a small plantation of larch and pine on your right, you will come to another track on your left. This leads to the stream at the bottom of the valley and the beautiful old stone bridge of Pont-Scethin that crosses it.

634236

It is difficult to imagine the London coach going over this bridge, but it must have done so. The overhanging bodywork of the coach would have lurched and swayed violently as the horses pulled up the approach to the steep arch of the bridge. Once you've crossed you will find that the traces of the old coaching road are much clearer. It goes a little way down the valley to the east, and then starts to wind up the southern heights. Here, beside the old road, you will see a remarkable stone. It was set up by Melvyn Haigh, sometime Bishop of Winchester, in memory of his mother Janet, who died in 1953. The tablet records that 'Even as late as her eighty-fourth year, despite dim sight and stiffened joints', that remarkable lady 'still loved to walk this way'. Her valiant spirit and love for this countryside lived on in her son, who will be long remembered in Dolgellau for his battles with unimaginative authorities and philistine planners. 'It was Dr Haigh', they will tell you, 'who got the telephone wires by Cader Idris laid under the ground.'

Even though you haven't climbed far out of the valley by the time you reach Janet Haigh's stone, you'll find that, on a bright day, you can see the Snowdon range from here and the mountains of Lleyn. I hope Janet was able to enjoy them in more than memory when she took her last walk this way.

Emergency shoeing station and cottage at Llety Loegr, last overnight shelter before going over the hills to Bontddu

From this point, where her stone wishes you 'Courage traveller', you can follow the old coach road over the ridge to the lane above Bontddu. Most of the droves, however, would not have climbed the hill here. They would have gone west along the banks of the Ysgethin to the track which runs through the pass of Bwlch y Rhiwgyr. Although this westerly track from Pont-Scethin runs through marshy ground it is fairly well defined, and for that you must thank the fishermen who come regularly

99

to the two lakes of this valley.

Going west from Pont-Scethin the track passes the northern shore of Llyn Irddyn. To the west of that lake it becomes even more clearly marked, and brings you to the ancient way leading to the pass. The tracks meet just south of another old bridge over the Ysgethin. This is Pont-Fadog, which carries a stone marking its date as 1762. The stone is also inscribed with the letters S A E R, which probably stand for the word 'craftsman',

in which case they give proper credit to this bridge's builder.

If you have time to make some extra walks in this area, it is certainly worth crossing Pont-Fadog and completing the circular walk back to Pont-Scethin. Immediately after you have crossed over the bridge, you will find Llety Loegr on your right. This is a holiday cottage now but its name, which means 'the English shelter', signifies that it was once an overnight stopping place for the drovers. It was also an emergency shoeing station.

Above Janet Haigh's stone
Left Pont-Scethin

It was probably here that the drovers from Cwm Nantcol joined the Bron-y-foel herds, before setting out to cross the pass together. The way you will now be walking is the way that the beasts from Bron-y-foel would have been brought. Follow the made-up road from Llety Loegr, past the cap-stone of a burial chamber which lies on your left in a small clump of hawthorn bushes. It is called Arthur's Quoit, and must be one of many stones whose unusual siting has given rise to the story that they were flung there by some hero of epic strength – in this case the

Left Llyn Irddyn
Below left Arthur's Quoit
Below Marker stone, London to Harlech road

legendary King Arthur.

This road brings you to a gateway. When you get through it you will find another gate immediately to your right. Beyond that is a very clear paved causeway, happily quite unfit for cars. You will have no trouble in following it round the hillside, although after some way the ancient pavings disappear and you are left with a muddy and sometimes boggy track. Just before you reach a gate set in a stone wall, you will find that another track goes

60223

Above Pont-Fadog

off to the left.

The left-hand way also leads through a gate, and the path beyond it takes you back to Bron-y-foel. If you keep to the main track and go through the gate on your right, you will come back to Pont-Scethin.

To return to the main way south from Pont-Fadog and the pass of Bwlch y Rhiwgyr (see map E). The path to the east of the bridge runs directly south-east. As you climb up it you will have a stone wall on your right and will pass the entrance to another cottage. As the track leaves these marks of habitation for the open hills it remains fairly clear and, unless the clouds are low, you will find that the notch of the pass between the hills is

Above The pass, Bwlch y
Rhiwgyr
Left Tal-y-bont to Bontddu
path, near Pont-Fadog

Far left Scots pines above Pont-
Fadog
Top left Tal-y-bont to Bontddu
path, near Bontddu

View back from Bwlch y
Rhiwgyr towards Pont-Fadog

continually in sight. When I first came this way, I met a walker
who had been visiting in the next valley towards Barmouth,
who assured me that this was not the ancient roadway. I
imagine that he felt the title properly belonged to the old
London to Harlech road. But I think he was wrong. The old
track you are on now was probably in existence long before
either of those places were built, and before there was any
thought of wheeled traffic through these hills. You will see
when you get to the narrow pass that it would be quite
impossible for any wheeled vehicle, other than a bicycle, to get
through it.

The old track takes you past the old mine workings on the
slopes of Llanaber to your right. Once you are past them you

Left Looking towards Cader Idris
Below Ruins of Golodd

are high enough to be able to look back, as John Roberts must have done, to take a last look at Llandanwg. From here, if the visibility is good and the tide is low, you will see the natural causeway running westwards through the bay. Some will tell you that this was the old road to Ireland, in the days when men were giants.

When you turn back to the east, you will find that you have a short, steep climb to the pass. Once you have gone through it you must decide whether to take the right-hand track that goes fairly steeply down the hillside to Barmouth or whether to stay with the drove way to the east. That track goes to the left along the steep side of Llawlech, and then gradually descends to the valley, skirting the Forestry Commission's litter of conifers, which ruin the southern side of this valley.

After a while the track crosses a stream, and runs east to the high ground of Uwch-mynydd. Just as you pass a small, steep earthwork on your right, and before you reach the lane that runs to Bontddu, you will come to an ancient milestone. This was probably put in place by the Romans, although the inscriptions are much later. The surface of the stone facing you informs you that Tal-y-bont, the village at the foot of the hill from Llety Loegr, is five miles (eight kilometres) away. On the back of the stone the distance to Harlech is given as eleven miles (17.7 kilometres).

From this old milestone you have a choice. There is no doubt that the droves would have followed the lane down to Bontddu. If you do so too, you should leave this lane where it crosses a stream and follow the public footpath sign, which directs you to 667198 the old gold mines. These drew their share of hopeful prospectors at the turn of the century, but their output was only just about enough to make wedding rings for the Royal Family. Although the mines were only developed towards the end of the nineteenth century, gold has been worked in this area intermittently from Roman times. The first miners could well have been descendants of the Stone Age people who settled around Moelfre, for the English meaning of Dolgellau is 'meadow of the slaves', which suggests that it was here that the Romans kept their labour force. From the mines, the path goes down to the main Barmouth to Dolgellau road.

For the writer John Ruskin, this road along the Mawddach estuary was the most beautiful walk in the world. Sadly that is not so today. It is overhung with pine trees, and the constant stream of cars along it in summer make it almost impassable for anyone on foot.

There is a way to avoid it, but it follows a fairly craggy ridgeway, and you should probably only try it in good weather unless you are a very experienced hill-walker. From the old milestone you must take the track running to the north of the Bontddu lane. After you have gone a little way you will find a path running east. This path, having crossed a stream, goes over the southern tip of a hill and into the next valley. Once you have gone over the Afon Cwm-llechen you will find the path climbs steeply to the rocks of Clogau. Just before you come to the eastern edge of that ridge, you will find a track running down the hill to your right. It winds narrowly through the heather to bring you about half-way down the hillside. Do not follow it through to the valley, but take the left-hand path here. That will lead you to a gate in a stone wall, leading into a pretty beech wood.

658206

When the path divides again, take the right-hand track. This will lead you downhill along the steep banks of the Cwm-mynach, past a roofless stone cottage and, after about ten minutes' further walking, to the main road at the village of Pen-y-bryn. Opposite you is the modern toll bridge that goes over the Mawddach for Dolgellau and Tywyn. On foot it will cost you 1p to cross (cars are 10p), and as you pay you can understand why the drovers were so determined to keep their animals on ways that were free of the tolls. If it is a clear day when you cross, and the tide is out, you will see on your right the strange sight of today's cattle basking on the sands.

690192

Once over the bridge don't make for the main Dolgellau to Tywyn road. Instead turn to your left through the old station yard until you come to the track, now devoid of sleepers and quite passable, if you don't mind walking for about a mile and a half (2.4 kilometres) on the stony railway bed. Just past the place where the old railway crosses the River Wnion, you can leave it by a stile on your right. Then cross over the stile on your left, and you will find yourself on the footpath that runs

714184

along the top of an earthwork by the river bank. This will lead you to a footbridge across the river and into the town of Dolgellau. Then, if you've managed the time correctly and the wind is in the right direction, you will be irresistibly led by the nose to Dolgellau's Baker Street. This narrow road is entirely taken up by a single bakery, and the bread and buns are lifted from the oven for you.

Although Dolgellau had a big April fair and market, and was an important gathering place for the cattle, it seems to have lacked a smith and for long periods was dependent on those from Bala. In 1925, when tales of the drovers were still vivid in people's minds, Hugh Evans recounted the following Dolgellau shoeing incident for the journal *Y Brython* (July 2nd):

At three in the morning, two blacksmiths, a feller (or over-thrower) and a helper started from Bala eighteen miles away carrying with them 480 shoes (cw in Welsh) and the necessary nails, hammers and knives. On reaching Dolgellau they set to work. The feller and his helper threw a rope round the bullock's horns; while the feller gripped the horns, the helper took hold of one foreleg, bending it at the joint. Then the feller twisted the horns and down went the bullock, being held firm while the helper bound its legs. A piece of iron about three feet [91 centimetres] long with a point at one end and a fork at the other was pushed into the ground, the point downward and the rope from the forelegs to the hindlegs was placed in the fork. The bullock was then ready to be shod. The first blacksmith trimming the hoof and the second nailing on the shoes. The bullocks were from two-and-a-half to three years old and hard to throw. One of them, a huge black steer from Anglesey, actually dragged the feller and his helper through the river; they held fast however and in the end 'Merionethshire had Anglesey down on his back'. The master blacksmith got 10d for each steer shod.

It must have been money well earned.

One may wonder what the Anglesey steer was doing so far south. Most of the cattle from the island would have been driven along the roads running north-east from Bangor and so to Wrexham. Yet that episode serves to remind us that

Llyn Cwm Bychan

cattle-droving, like any other agricultural activity, never took place on a uniformly standard pattern. It is tempting to think that there were other routes out of the Harlech dome, besides the old tracks to the south; and there does seem to be evidence that some cattle were driven east, over the old pack-horse tracks that cross the mountains lying between Ardudwy and the Eden valley to the south of Trawsfynydd. Because they are so beautiful, it would be sad to leave this part of Wales without walking along these mountain paths.

If you intend to do so it would be helpful, but not essential, to join up with somebody with a car who didn't want to follow the whole walk. Otherwise you are going to find yourself walking along eight miles (12.8 kilometres) of metalled lane, some of which you will have already travelled when you started out to reach the old London to Harlech road from Cwm Nantcol.

Map F page 117 For the round walk, take the lane that runs north-east from Llanbedr to Cwm Bychan. The way to this strange remote valley, in which some people report the same sense of evil that lurks in the Dolbenmaen Mountains to the north, can get very crowded during the holiday season. If there is anything eerie here, the picnickers who make the day excursion to Llyn Cwm Bychan certainly dispel it. The farmer who lives at the end of

this valley has turned the field at the eastern end of the lake into a car park for the day trippers. Beyond that field, a sign-post on your right directs you to the Roman steps. Although this partly paved track to the mountain pass is called Roman, it is likely that the path existed long before the legions came to Wales and that the pavings of the steps are actually medieval. So 'Roman' is a good mean dating.

You walk for a little way through a wood before you come to the steps themselves. Once clear of the wood the path, which forms into steps at its steepest points, runs clearly up to the cairn that marks the pass.

Just before you reach the neck of the pass, and before the cairn comes in sight, you may be able to see a raven's nest on a high ledge to the west. In late May and early June, when the young are nearly full-grown and constantly demanding food, you can sometimes see them quite clearly from the path. And on this western side of the mountain, even in August with many people about, you can still catch glimpses of the beautiful black and white wild goats which live in these crags. There are reckoned to be about 100 to 150 goats wintering in Cwm Bychan and climbing higher into the hills in summer. They are not popular with the local farmers, for they do a certain amount of damage to the dry stone walls, and in a drought year, when grazing is short, they take valuable food away from the sheep. However, for 'old time's sake' a certain number of them will always be tolerated here.

When you reach the cairn at the top of this pass you will find that the path fades for a while, but as you go down the mountainside you can see the western part of the Coed y Brenin Forest below you. Keep the crags on your right until you come to the path that leads into the forest.

For the circular walk you should turn right when you reach the Forestry Commission road. However, if you have time to spare, it is worth turning left a little way and then following the paths running east until you come clear of the forest. Once you get beyond the trees, on the slopes of Crawcwellt, you will find a track running north-east to the farm of Adwy-dêg. From here several paths run north towards Trawsfynydd. In this country

646315

Llyn Cwm Bychan

657300

670298

695314

which lies between Trawsfynydd and Bronaber to the south, it is still possible to find discarded ox cues – a sign that cattle were once brought over these steep mountain passes from the Harlech dome.

Mr Martin Allinson, who farms at Trawsfynydd and to whom I am indebted for my information on this area, has a good tale to tell about a legendary Trawsfynydd smith. This giant of a man went along with the drovers in order to attend to the cattle on the route. But his main role was quite different. He was there to provide entertainment, and he was put up to fight the champions of other groups of drovers at the various inns on the way. But however the bets were laid, no fight ever took place.

The giant smith squeezed his opponent's hand so hard as a friendly gesture before the contest that, in Mr Allinson's words, 'the opposition was incapacitated immediately.'

To return to the circular walk. Go south through Coed y Brenin Forest, but do not go so far south that you cross the Afon Gau. Just before you get to that stream turn to your right, and head west until you come out of the wood and find the great mountain of Rhinog Fawr on your right. The path you are now 665283 on will climb to a pass to the north of the gentler heights of Rhinog Fach. The pass is marked by a large cairn.

Once past the cairn on your way to the west, a series of smaller cairns mark the path for your descent. In many ways this path is even more beautiful and certainly less frequented than the Roman steps. There are steps here too, and they probably have the same history as those on the more northerly pass.

In late July and August the slopes of the mountains here are covered in bilberries, which your motorized friends, who hopefully will have driven along Cwm Nantcol to meet you, can spend the waiting time collecting. They should, however, only pick those that grow on the lower slopes, for as you will notice parts of this path run through a nature reserve, which means that growing things as well as animal life must not be disturbed by visitors. The path brings you to the lane which ends at this 642269 eastern extremity of Cwm Nantcol. At this point you will see another footpath running due north into the mountains past a

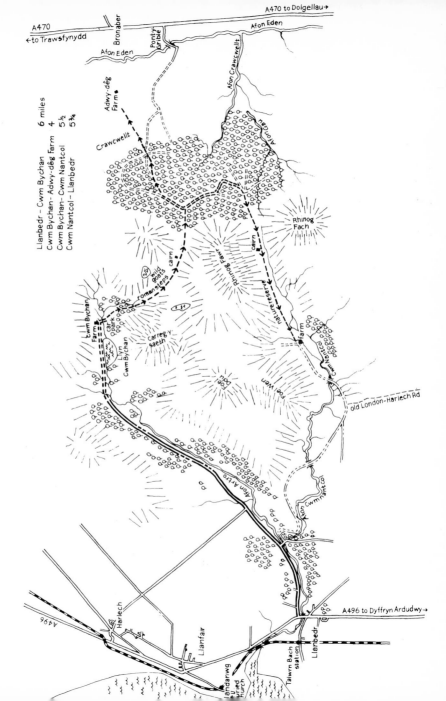

Map F

A470 to Doigellau→

A470

←to Trawsfynydd

Bronaber

Afon Eden

Pont-y-faribie

Afon Eden

Afon Crawcwellt

Afon Eden

Adwy-dég Farm

Crawcwellt

Afon Gau

Rhinog Fach

wild goats

cairn

cairn

Rhinog Fawr

roman steps

Cwm Bychan Farm

car park

Carreg-y-saeth

Llyn Cwm Bychan

nature reserve

Farm

Cwm Nantcol

Moel y Blithcwm

Moel Wern

old London-Harlech Rd

Afon Artro

Afon Cwm-nantcol

A496 to Dyffryn Ardudwy→

Harlech

Llanfair

A496

Talwrn Bach station

Llanbedr

Llandanwg ruined church

Llanbedr – Cwm Bychan   6 miles
Cwm Bychan- Adwy-dég Farm   4
Cwm Bychan– Cwm Nantcol   5½
Cwm Nantcol – Llanbedr   5¾

N

lonely farm house. You might imagine that this way would take you to the Roman steps, but it does not do so. It leads to some beautiful mountain walks, but they do not properly belong to this story.

Our main journey now runs north-east from Dolgellau to Bala. At the time of the toll gates the Ardudwy drovers would not have been keen to take their herds of cattle and flocks of sheep directly to Bala, along the road that the blacksmith used. So many of them would have turned north off that road, which follows the eastern course of the Wnion as it leaves Dolgellau, 754224 and so made their way to the village of Llanfachreth. You can reach that village now by taking the main Bala road out of Dolgellau, and then walking along the lane on your left that is sign-posted to it.

It is from Llanfachreth that one gets some estimate of the sort of money that was involved in the cattle transactions of the late eighteenth century. The figures are taken from a drover's account book published by Mr K. Williams-Jones in the *Proceedings of the Merioneth Historical Record Society* for 1956. In this case the drover, whose name was John Williams, was not himself a dealer. He drove cattle for a Mr Garrions, an important landowner in the area, who might have been a relation of that John Garrions of Rhiw-goch who, with his son Griffith, acted as a clerk of the peace for Merioneth from 1751 to 1783. John Williams himself was a man of some substance and, droving being a part-time occupation, he was able to combine it as many of his fellows did with running an ale house in his home village. His accounts detail the expenses that he incurred in driving the cattle from Bala to Billerkey (Billericay) in Essex and the prices he realized on the sale of the beasts. The entire cost of the project was £47 17s, but the actual expenses for the journey only amounted to £26 10s. The difference was spent in England at Brentwood Fair, and on lodging for the men and grazing for the cattle at Epping and Coldhill. The cost of the return journey for John Williams and his mare was 16s. On the credit side he sold forty runts for £120; twenty for £54; ten for £28 10s; sixteen for £32; as well as twenty-four calves for £1 each and three cows for £7 3s. He also got rid of two of the horses that he had used on the journey, selling the black one for £2 12s and the white one for a guinea.

Visit Llanfachreth church before you follow John Williams and Mr Garrions's cattle through the pass to the north of the village and on to the road for Bala. A tombstone here will give you a quick lesson in the way that Welsh names were handed down through the generations, the son being christened with the father's surname. This may help to clear up some of the confusions you are bound to encounter. The stone commemorates 'Catherine, daughter of Lewis Williams, the son of William Lewis, who died at the residence of her brother William Lewis Cadwgan. February 13th, 1875. Aged 31.' This church is also notable for the pious tributes, one in Welsh and one in English, on its lychgate, which praise George III, the farmer king. These slates were set up by Sir Robert Williams Vaughan of Nannau, whose family owned most of the land in the area.

It was Sir Robert who caused the present church to be built in the early nineteenth century, because the one that Mr Garrions would have known had become too small for its congregation. Mr Garrions and John Williams would find the lychgate familiar though, for it was from that point that the bell-ringer gave out the important farming news to the village. Standing on the high, stone mounting-block he informed the village of the dates of the Dolgellau fairs, and announced what the local farmers would have to contribute in taxes for the destruction of foxes. In those years there was no prohibition on Sabbath-day drinking; after the church services, the people crossed the road to the farm house of Ty-isa, in whose cellars the main brewing for the village was done.

The church is dedicated to Machreth (mutations often occur in Welsh place names). He was a Celtic saint, who is popularly believed to have lived some time in the fifth century. The legend is that he dwelt in the woods above the church, where the farm of Gellfachreth (the hiding place of Machreth) now stands. Another Celtic saint, Gwynnog, is reported to have stayed with the saint and blessed the village well, whose waters were thought to have healing powers right up to the 1920s.

Map G page 121 A few yards along the road running east from the church is the village school. A public footpath directs you through the woods that run along its westerly side. This track is an almost classic drove way, with clear banks on either side of it. It ends at a gate, 763226 on the other side of which are two public footpath signs. One directs you straight into the woods. If you follow it you will come out by the climb to the mountain pass. The other sends you to the right, past two farm houses, one of which is extremely old and built in the traditional long house pattern, whereby the family dwelling section and the cattle byres formed one continuous whole.

This path takes you across two fields and on to a farm road, 766232 marked on the Ordnance Survey maps as Cors-y-garnedd. You turn left here and walk up hill until you come to a gate. Once through the gate the track becomes much rougher, and at the point where it crosses the River Lâs (a fairly narrow stream) you will see that it is joined on the left by the track that you would have come out on, had you followed the path through th

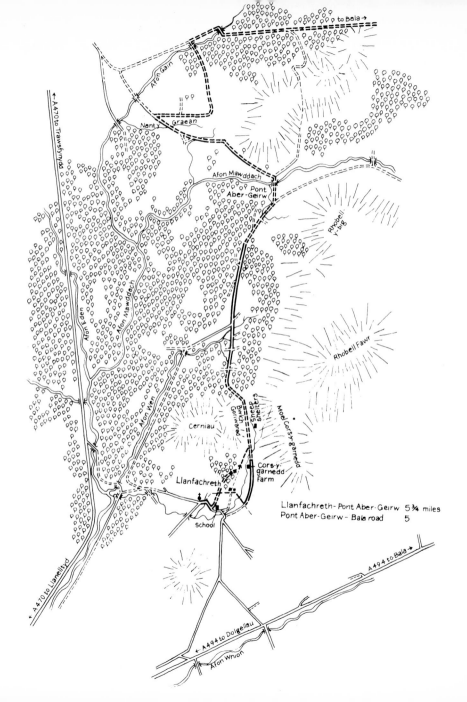

Map G

N

← A470 to Trawsfynydd

to Bala →

Afon Gain

Nant y Graean

Afon Mawddach

Pont Aber-Geirw

Rhobell y Big

Rhobell Fawr

Afon Eden

Afon Mawddach

Afon Wen

Bwlch Goriwaered

Sheep shelters

Moel Cors-y-garnedd

Cerniau

Cors-y-garnedd Farm

Llanfachreth

Llanfachreth- Pont Aber-Geirw   5¾ miles
Pont Aber-Geirw - Bala road   5

School

← A470 to Llanelltyd

A494 to Bala →

← A494 to Dolgellau

Afon Wnion

Above Llanfachreth

woods instead of going past the farms. The track now heads for the pass, Bwlch Goriwared, which takes you between the fairly gentle hills of Cerniau to the west and the crags of Moel Cors-y-garnedd to the east. On the heights of the pass, beneath the rocks on your right, are some ruined sheep shelters.

765245   From the pass you can look down, as John Williams would have done, on to the Mawddach valley. Perhaps it was here that another Llanfachreth drover, Thomas Williams of Pennard Wnion Fawr, first decided to give up the wandering life and planned the bookselling and printing business which he is said to have eventually owned. (Unfortunately, I cannot find any precise information about Williams's second career, but the story seems authentic, and is in line with many others which illustrate the keen interest which the drovers showed in the world at large.) Certainly neither of these drovers would expect to see the plantations of pines that now obscure the moors and pockets of woodland that marked the start of their journey to the east. Mountains don't change so much though. The two high hills in the east are Rhobell-y-big to the north and Rhobel

Fawr to the south. The story goes that Saint Machreth once had to flee from his own village and take refuge in a cave in these mountains. Here the faithful came to join him in worshipping the persecuted God. Parts of these mountains were officially known as 'the old church' until the beginning of this century.

A word of warning. As you walk through the country here, keep to well-defined tracks and to the roads that run through the plantations. This is not just because the ground landlords of Llechweddgain Common are particularly strict about trespassers, but more urgently because this was once a War Defence firing range. So you are frequently warned, 'Do not touch anything. It may explode and kill you.'

So once you have gone north over the pass, it's best to keep to the forest path running through the eastern edge of Coed y Brenin. This will bring you out to the bridge of Pont Aber-Geirw, where you turn left and walk about four miles (6.4 kilometres) to the north-west. Then take the road on your right, which brings you to the mountain road for Bala by a small bridge crossing the Afon Gain. Turn right and cross the river again at a point where the road enters forest land once more. After you've walked east for about a mile (1.6 kilometres) through these trees, you will see a track running down to the south. It goes across the hills to Pont Aber-Geirw, and no doubt that was the way that the drovers would have come north from the Mawddach, before explosives had to be considered.

768291

736307

765330

The drove ways that lie to the north of this road in the wild area between Trawsfynydd and Bala are given in the Porthmadog section on pages 74-8.

To reach Bala you must carry on to the east until, about half a mile (804 metres) after the lane crosses the River Lliw, you find a track going straight ahead into the hills at a point where the lane turns to the south-east. After some four miles (6.4 kilometres) this track crosses the Afon Dylo and joins a farm lane. When it divides turn right and at the minor road turn left, and keep going east. It will bring you on to the A road running along the northern shore of Bala Lake about three miles (4.8 kilometres) from the town.

811335

854342

888324

Bala consists of one wide, busy main street. There are water sports on its lake, and as it is also a convenient centre for the mountains it is packed with visitors in the holiday months. It has always been of some importance, both as a meeting place and shoeing station for the drovers and as a centre for the marketing of woollen goods. Before the flannel mills kept the weavers working in Newtown and Llanidloes, Welsh wool was knitted into stockings, which were regularly sold at special markets as far away as Farnham in Surrey. The drovers who acted as messengers in so many ways probably took woollen goods from the western farms to sell in Bala.

For many years the farm economy was partly geared to the output of knitted garments, particularly stockings. In winter evenings both men and women got down to this work, much of which was done in the dark, for candles were expensive and the life of a rush light was brief. The farm kitchen which has been put together in the museum at Brecon, and those that you can see in the restored farm houses in the open air museum at St Fagans outside Cardiff, give you some idea of the conditions in which the work was carried out.

By the end of the eighteenth century, people had another reason to walk over the upland moors to Bala. It was the home of Thomas Charles, an ordained priest of the established Church, who became an ardent Methodist. He founded the Sunday School Movement in Wales and the British and Foreign Bible Society, as a direct result of his desire to improve the education of the poor and to make the Bible in Welsh available to every family. There are many stories of the heroic barefoot tramps that were undertaken in order to obtain copies of the precious book. And Bala is still a literary town, with a bookshop well-stocked with poetry in Welsh and English. Hugh Jones and John Thomas, Bala drovers who were among the subscribers to the eighteenth-century *Wales Golden Treasury*, would no doubt not think it so odd that the birthplace of Taliesin's mother should still find an audience for verse.

Bala/Llangollen

(Ordnance Survey sheet 125)

Almost every drover in Wales went through Corwen at one time
or another. It was there that most of the beasts who had been
driven from Ardudwy and the Harlech dome to Bala joined up
with the droves from Anglesey and the Lleyn peninsula. From
there they went east towards Llangollen, Wrexham and
Shrewsbury.

The way from Bala lay along the north and west banks of the
Dee, through Llandderfel, and from there across country to
Druid or directly alongside the river to Corwen. You can get a
bus today from Bala to Llandderfel; as this is rather a busy
road, and as there are no alternative ways of walking, you would
be wise to do so.

982370   For the nineteenth-century drovers, Llandderfel must have
been mostly noted as the home of Robert Roberts, whose
memorial stone in the disused and broken down churchyard
tells today's visitors that he was a 'farrier and herbalist who for
thirty years served the neighbourhood in the useful capacity of
veterinary surgeon'. He died in 1852 at the age of sixty; so he
would have been known to the children of the National School
of 1828, now a private house, which stands in the little town
square where the bus stops.

Map H page 126   To reach Corwen from the town square you must take the
minor road running east, and either follow it along by the river
or leave it almost immediately by a lane that climbs steeply up
to your left. This way will take you along the ridgeway path,
and will reward you with a view of the Berwyn to the east.

995384   When this lane becomes a farm track, keep to the right-hand

125

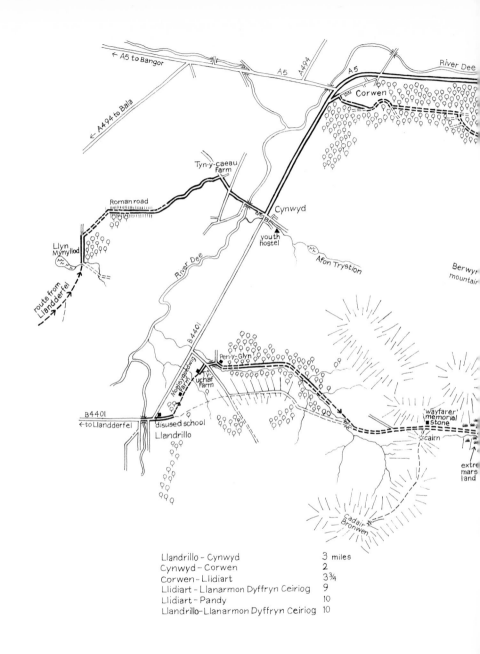

N

← A5 to Bangor

A5

A494

A5

River Dee

Corwen

← A494 to Bala

Tyn-y-caeau Farm

Cynwyd

Roman road

youth hostel

Afon Tryslion

Berwyn mountain

Llyn Mynyllod

River Dee

route from Llandderfel

B4401

Pen-y-Glyn

Moelypepdwg farm

Uchaf Farm

'wayfarer' memorial stone

B4401

← to Llandderfel

disused school

Llandrillo

cairn

extreme marsh land

Cadair Bronwen

Llandrillo – Cynwyd	3 miles
Cynwyd – Corwen	2
Corwen – Llidiart	3¾
Llidiart – Llanarmon Dyffryn Ceiriog	9
Llidiart – Pandy	10
Llandrillo – Llanarmon Dyffryn Ceiriog	10

rog

Owen
Glyndwrs
Tump

Llidiart

A 5 to Llangollen →

Nant y Pandy

sused
arry

stile

Plasnewydd

nel Fferna

old quarry

Berwyn mountains

Ceriog Ddu

Ceriog
Forest

Plas Nantyr

B 4500 to Chirk →

Pen
plaenau

ing

Waterfalls

Pandy

gate

Tu-hwnt-ir-afon
Farm

B 4500

Llanarmon
Dyffryn Ceiriog

path which climbs over Mynydd Mynyllod and runs by the eastern tip of Llyn Mynyllod. There you reach a piece of woodland. Turn north along its western side, until you reach the end of the wood, where you join the ridgeway path running to the north-east. Follow this until you have passed another small stretch of woodland. At this point you will come to a gate on your right leading to a farm lane. This lane, which runs steeply down hill and then goes due east in an absolutely straight line for about a quarter of a mile (402 metres), is one of the few stretches of Roman road in Wales not to run north/south. Several pieces of Roman pottery and carved stones have been found by the farmers who own the neighbouring fields.

018402

026414

The present metalled lane has wide verges and the width between the banks, which at some stage were planted with hawthorn, suggests that it must have been a major thorough-fare in its time. Certainly the droves would have made good use of it.

This bit of straight road soon gets lost in a winding lane. When this lane meets a minor road you can either turn left for Druid and Corwen, or you can turn right for the bridge across the Dee. The latter course will bring you to the village of Cynwyd, where the Youth Hostel stands in the small square to the east of the little bridge across the Afon Trystion.

Owen Glendower's Tump

The road from Cynwyd to Corwen runs along the eastern banks of the Dee. From Corwen you can go east along the A5 or along the forestry paths that run parallel to it, until you reach the village of Llidiart. Just opposite the telephone box you will see a 'No Through Road' which climbs the hillside into the forest. This path will take you across the Berwyn, for the route to Shrewsbury.

118433

The public footpath sign which you will see on your right after you have walked a little way along this path directs you to some tracks of a disused quarry and then through Cynwyd Forest land to Corwen. This is where you would have come out if you had taken the forest paths above the A5. The way south lies up the hill. The forestry road climbs in wide bends; but there is one point where it is interesting to leave it. When the road first swings round to the left, you will see a small clearing straight ahead of you going directly up the hill. This track must surely have been the old road to the mountains. It crosses a stream twice, and those causeways and its old pavings indicate that it was once a highway. At one point its way is blocked by a large flat rock.

This track brings you out again on to the forest road, which you follow to its highest point. Here you will find steps built over the wire fence that divides the forest from the open mountain. There is

122416
aterfall on Ceiriog Ddu stream

no easily visible track across the rather swampy ground to the south, where the way runs along the eastern side of Moel Fferna. But the path running on slightly higher ground and further to the east can be easily traced. This path climbs round

124400   the side of a hill, and then descends quite steeply to a farm lan If you turn right here you come to some old quarry roads and the track going south by the stream of Ceiriog Ddu. Go along

137348   beside the stream, past the waterfall, to the farm of Tu-
157328   hwnt-i'r-afon and the lane to Llanarmon Dyffryn Ceiriog.

The other route to that village goes through Ceiriog Forest. If you turn left at Plasnewydd, away from the old quarries, you will come to a track on your right running downhill to the stream of Nant y Pandy. When you have crossed the stream

146414   take the track to your left to climb the hillside a little way, an then turn due south to Ceiriog Forest. Keep going south along the tracks through this forest, until you emerge on the western slopes of a hill. Go round this hill through another short stretc

160373   of woodland until you meet a lane. Turn left here and follow t lane for about a mile and a half (2.4 kilometres), until you com

185370   to the third lane running off on your left. Immediately opposit this you will find the track for Pandy, marked 'Unfit for Moto Vehicles'. This hollow way, which becomes a steep path throug the woods, crosses the River Teirw and runs along its west side

195358   You come out by Pandy church on the road that runs between Llanarmon Dyffryn Ceiriog and Chirk.

This point can also be reached by a more southerly route acros the Berwyn, and this was the way that many of the drovers, who had no need to pass through Corwen, would have gone. It

035371   starts from the busy droving centre of Llandrillo, which lies to the east of Llandderfel across the Dee.

You start out from Llandrillo along the main road to Corwen, but just after you have crossed the bridge in the town, you will

036373   see a disused school building beside a 'No Through Road' which runs eastwards. Follow this lane, keeping always to the left and ignoring any right-hand turns, until you reach the gate of Tyn-y Cae. Here the road ends and on your right yo will find a gate leading to a woodland path that runs north-eas along the side of the hill above Moelisygoedwig Farm.

emains of old fence on Ceiriog
du stream

When the path comes clear of the wooded stretch it is joined by a farm track which runs up the hill. Ignore this and keep with the fainter path that goes round the side of the hill, with a hedge on your left. Soon the marks of the old track that was once a busy drove way become quite clear, although they are lost where a clump of gorse has grown up in the path. Once past the gorse the traces resume again, and the path leads to a causeway crossing a stream.

When you have crossed the stream, you will see a path running up the hill to your right and going through some woodland. Inviting as it is, it must be ignored, for the drove way goes through the gate into a field. The path stays to the right of the dividing hedge, and shows every sign of being an ancient green lane. It comes out by the farm of Tŷ-uchaf.

046383   When the farm road meets a lane, turn right. Ignore the first turn off it on the right and follow the lane to the left over a little bridge; then turn right by the cottage of Pen-y-Glyn,

along the lane to Blaen-y-glyn. The track is now running through woodland, the pines occasionally interspersed with larches and with blackberries and raspberries thick on its verges. At the end of the wood a gate brings you out on to the hill, with the forest itself extending on your right.

068375

The path goes along the side of a hill parallel to the northern edge of this tongue of pines. When you come opposite the end of the forest you will see a track going down to a stream on your

Above and left On the road between Llandrillo and Llanarmon Dyffryn Ceiriog

right. It is worth going along it a little way for the sake of the lovely old stone bridge across the stream, but the track on the other side of it simply leads back to Moelisygoedwig. The eastward track carries on along the side of the hill, and then starts to climb steadily towards a pass, which is marked by a cairn on the southern summit. From that cairn a hilltop path runs due south to the summit of Cadair Bronwen.

091366

Just to the north of the pass to Nant Rhydwylim, a stone is let into the rock in memory of 'Wayfarer', a lover of Wales and particularly of these mountains. This brief memorial conceals the identity of an intrepid cyclist, W. M. Robinson. John Hunt, who succeeded him on the Council when he retired from the Cyclist Touring Club in 1947, and who is a member of the Rough Stuff Fellowship, told me how that organization – founded after Robinson's death – was responsible for the erection of the stone. The R.S.F. is an association of cyclists who love the byways, and Mr Hunt believes that it owes its existence to Robinson's 'writings and lectures and his constant plea to get off the beaten track, even to the extent of carrying our bicycles over the shoulders on mountain passes.' He lived from 1877 to 1956.

By Robinson's stone is a metal box. It is not somebody's forgotten lunch tin, so open it. Inside you will find an exercise book in which people who pass this way are asked to write their names.

This path running east through the pass is locally known as the Maids' Path, for this is the way that girls used to come at harvest time, walking east from Llandrillo to seek work in the next valley. They would have had swampy lands to cover, but old railway sleepers have now been used to make a firm path across the marshes. At the eastern end of the marshes, you will see stones on the hill to your left. These mark the way to Pen-plaenau and the mountains of the north.

The Maids' Path then crosses a stream by an ugly modern bridge and runs through lovely country, following the southern bank of a stream, and so to a gate which leads to the lane for Llanarmon Dyffryn Ceiriog, an exceptionally pretty mountain village. From there you can either go east to Chirk, or make your way north to finish the drovers' story at Llangollen. This town is now famous for two things: the two ladies who eloped together from Ireland to hold court there and the present-day annual International Eisteddfod. To the nineteenth-century Shropshire farmers, however, it meant something quite different. This was where they came to buy pigs and cattle, and a good price they paid for them. In George Borrow's time the pigs were changing hands at eighteen to twenty shillings. Parting with the money was not all the purchaser had to worry about. Pigs are the least tractable of domestic animals, and Borrow reports that 'dire was the screaming of the porkers, yet the purchaser invariably seemed to know how to manage his bargain, keeping the left arm round the body of the swine and with the right hand fast grasping the ear – some few are led away by strings.'[4]

The Way to Birmingham
Llanidloes and the Kerry Ridgeway

(Ordnance Survey sheet 136)

The cattle which converged on the market town of Llanidloes from the mountainous region that lies between Machynlleth and Staylittle, to the north of Llangurig, traversed the most ancient part of Wales. Both the basic rocks and the traces of human habitation in this area stretch further back than those of other regions. Centuries before the Celts came to Britain, men were living in these hills. Their descendants stayed on in their isolated settlements, having so little contact with the subsequent waves of invaders that physical anthropologists have noted that they have kept their distinctive features to this day, being much darker and swarthier than the Celts.

From Llanidloes the route follows the northerly course of the River Severn for a few miles, and then climbs into the mountains which lie to the east. This region is now bisected by the Newtown to Llandrindod Wells road. A couple of miles to the east of the road you will find the main meeting place for the Monmouthshire drovers. It is marked by the twin barrows (Two Tumps) which were raised at the western edge of the Kerry Ridgeway, and marked an important route long before men started moving cattle.

118851

This ancient track dominates a region of beef and dairy farming most of whose commerce is now conducted along the roads going north to Shrewsbury or south to Hereford.

From the Plynlimon Mountains, where both the Wye and the Severn start and whose rocks are older than those of the Alps, the Andes and the Himalayas, the sheep and cattle were brought down to the village of Llangurig and the market town of Llanidloes. Throughout history religion and trade have followed the same routes, and the cattle who were driven along this way from the north-west would have gone over the same mountain passes as Saint Curig and his followers, who came in the early sixth century to found the church that still carries his name. Like many other early missionaries to Britain, Curig came from Ireland and journeyed east from Cardigan Bay. He died on February 17th, 550, nearly half a century before Augustine established Christianity at Canterbury. The monastery or *clas* that he founded, where Llangurig stands now, flourished until the end of the twelfth century, when the community came under the dominion of the Cistercian Abbey of Strata Florida to the west.

In the next section of the book, the route to Llangurig from Cwmystwyth is described. It was shared by the monks of Strata Florida and the cattle dealers from the great fairs at Devil's Bridge and Ffair Rhos.

Map I page 139 The most northerly route in this area runs from Machynlleth to Staylittle, a tiny village in the hills just above the northern tip of Llyn Clywedog, some eight miles (12.8 kilometres) out of Llanidloes. You will need Ordnance Survey sheet 135 for this walk, which you can start by taking the train to Machynlleth. 745014 From the station turn south into the town, until you reach the main shopping street which runs east to Penegoes. The Owen Glendower Institute, on the site where his parliament was held, is on this street, a few yards down on your right-hand side.

Follow this main road until you come to the hospital, where you will find a minor road running off to the right. As the road leaves the town here it runs through a golf course, where both the scenery and the tilt of the land must lead to some fairly memorable games. This road goes on to the village of Forge, 763001 where you cross the bridge and follow the road along the northern bank of the Afon Dulas. This is a very beautiful road and not much frequented by cars, even in the height of the holiday season.

796985 If you are in a car yourself you can follow the drove route over Rhiw Fawr by taking the turning on your left, where the road climbs away from the river. Walkers will want to go a few yards

137

further along the road by the Dulas until it crosses a stream. At this point a track runs off to the left and runs south-east through a strip of forest land to the village of Aberhosan, where there is a post-office shop. Turn right along the road that runs

814974 through the village until it ends by some farm buildings. At this point the road becomes a lane and then a track which climbs quite steeply, then runs along the south side of a strip of forest

836959 to come out on the heights of the Machynlleth to Staylittle mountain road, to the south of Rhiw Fawr.

Another way to reach this road is to carry along the banks of the Dulas, and when the road clears the forest to follow straight

810962 ahead on the farm track to Nant y Fyda. The mountain path now climbs steeply to the pass between Foel Fadian and the

833948 crags of Uwch-y-coed. When it meets another track running across the level ground, turn left to join the mountain road.

When you reach the road turn right for Dylife. The drove track

847943 leaves the road on the right after a mile (1.6 kilometres) or so. It runs alongside a farm entrance, and goes by the banks of a pond to climb by a stretch of woodland to the summit of Penycroc-

856935 bren, where a Roman fort once stood. Its name means 'gibbet hill' and it was used as such during the eighteenth century and probably later. One of the men whose body hung there was Sion y Gof (John the Smith). He was a Cardiganshire man who, sometime around 1700, murdered his wife and children by throwing them down a deserted mine-shaft. Possibly his tragedy started when as a travelling smith he left the Cardiganshire droves for the Dylife lead mines with their promise of great wealth.

The way goes east over the hill, but it is worth leaving it for a little while by the track that winds down fairly steeply on your

8694 left towards Dylife village. This ghostly, deserted place was once a flourishing township, and during the eighteenth century the lead from here was taken by horse-drawn waggons along the mountain road to Machynlleth; no doubt they all too often found their way blocked by droves of cattle and sheep. In the mid-nineteenth century the mine belonged to the parents-in-law of Richard Cobden, the exponent of free trade and of the abolition of the corn laws that were causing widespread poverty

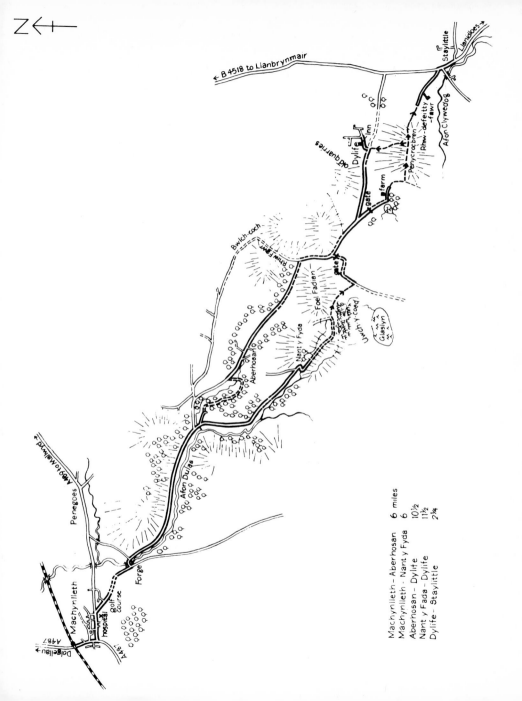

Map I

Machynlleth - Aberhosan   6 miles
Machynlleth - Nant y Fyda   6
Aberhosan - Dylife   10½
Nant y Fada - Dylife   11½
Dylife - Staylittle   2¾

at that time. When the old owners died, he obtained virtual control of the Dylife workings, and with his fellow reformer John Bright he formed a Manchester-based company in the late 1850s and bought the Dylife workings for £24,000.

They made radical improvements to the miners' conditions, and for years Dylife was the only mine in Wales and the north of England to provide changing rooms for the men. It is hard to believe now that over a thousand people lived here about a century ago and that there were three or four inns, a church, several chapels and a school to provide for their needs. Today only the Star Inn remains.

When they reached Dylife, the droves went to the right to climb the hilltops, along the track which you would now be wise to retrace. When you rejoin the hill track follow it to your left for a little way, and then it runs south-east towards the farm of

877932   Rhiw-defeitty-fawr. From this point a farm track descends to the road junction at the head of Llyn Clywedog. To your left the road runs to Newtown, to the right to Staylittle and Llanidloes. But any walker going to the latter town would do

884924   well to take the very sharp turn on the right and to go by the minor road, which runs through forest land and along the western shores of the lake.

Map J page 141 From this minor road you could also make your way west to Llangurig. In that case, when the forest road turns to the lake,

860892   go west to the farm of Cwmbiga and then follow the forest road south until it reaches the banks of the infant Severn. You will be able to cross the river when the road gets clear of the trees and climb up the track on the opposite side which runs south-west into another part of the forest. When you reach the

883852   road running east, follow it until it clears the trees, when you will find a path climbing almost due south. Follow this over the

882836   hills to meet a road which you cross. Go along a farm track here which runs south-east across Briwnant. When your path is crossed by a lane turn south to go along the western side of a

890813   valley, through a couple of fields beside the farm of Pen-y-foel. The farm track brings you into a narrow lane, and if you turn left along it you come to the main road, which runs along by the side of the Wye. Llangurig is about a mile (1.6 kilometres) to the east.

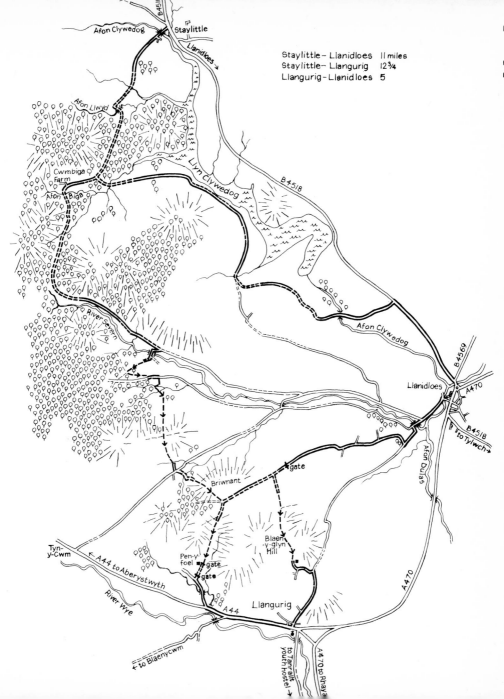

N

Map J

Afon Clywedog
Staylittle

Llanidloes

Staylittle – Llanidloes   11 miles
Staylittle – Llangurig   12¾
Llangurig – Llanidloes   5

Afon Llwyd

Llyn Clywedog

B4518

Cwmbiga
Farm

Afon Biga

River Severn

Afon Clywedog

B4569

Llanidloes

A470

B4518
to Tylwch →

gate

Briwnant

Afon Dulas

Blaen
-y-glyn
Hill

Tyn-
y-Cwm
← A44 to Aberystwyth

Pen-y-
foel   gate

gate

Llangurig

A470

River Wye

A44

← to Blaenycwm

to Tan'rallt
youth hostel →

A470 to Rhaya

The other way to reach this village is to go north-east, instead of dropping south to Pen-y-foel. This brings you to quite a sizeable farm track. When you find a cultivated field on your left (kale in 1976) and an old railway waggon used as a farm hut, you can either carry on along the track which will eventually bring you to Llanidloes or turn south over Blaen-y-glyn Hill. This brings you to a farm road which descends steeply to the stream. You pass the farm building, which is now used as a holiday cottage, on your left and then follow the lane until you reach the mountain road. You are now about a mile (1.6 kilometres) north of Llangurig. Turn right to reach the village which you will enter by the steep hill which runs alongside the Bluebell Inn.

833907

The Llangurig herds that were heading for the south (and not going up to Llanidloes) would have been driven towards Abbeycwmhir to join the herds going east from Rhayader. To follow their route you must take the main road from Llangurig to Llanidloes for about a mile and a half (2.4 kilometres), until you come to a lane on your right running to the village of Tylwch. This lane joins the B road where it crosses a bridge over the Dulas. An alternative way to join this road would be along the ridgeway of Creigiaullwydion, which you reach by taking the track that climbs to the right, a couple of miles along the Tylwch lane from the main Llanidloes road. The ridgeway track descends to the valley about a mile (1.6 kilometres) south of Tylwch. You can also reach Tylwch by the path on the left of the lane, which climbs Bryn Mawr and then heads due east.

933801
970801

951797

At 976784 a very sharp turn on your left takes you down to the Dulas and the ford where that river meets the Rhydydwydau Brook. There is now a small bridge across one of the fords, but there are still traces of the causeways fording both waters here. Tradition has it that this was an important collecting place for sheep that were being driven to the south, and its name – Rhyd-myheryn (the ford of the rams) – bears this out. If you cross it and follow the path climbing up to the forest, and then take the forest road going east, you will come out on the lane above Bwlch-y-sarnau and Abbeycwmhir.

The other way to leave the ford of the rams today is to walk due south along the old railway track which will bring you out opposite the post office in the village of Pant-y-dŵr. This is where the herds and flocks would have been met by those from the south, and you will find the route you should now follow in the next section on page 168.

To return to the route for the north. The mountain road from Llangurig to Llanidloes enters that town by Short Bridge Street, which was once a cattle market. In fact, so many animals were constantly changing hands at Llanidloes that in 1852 a proclamation was made in the town declaring that farmers and dealers must stop their beasts wandering unattended through the streets. By then the town was one of the main centres of the flannel industry, and commerce had to be given precedence over agriculture.

Today it is a popular tourist centre, and you will find that it is a good base for walks in the area. It is also an interesting place in its own right, with a lively and significant history, much of which is recorded in the town museum housed in the old market hall.

Llanidloes Market Hall

There you will find relics and documents relating to the riots of the spring of 1839, when the London police had to be called in to restore order to the town. The violent unrest that took place here was part of the general upheaval in mid-Wales at that time. In October 1838 at Newtown, to the north-east of Llanidloes, the first Chartist meeting in Wales was held. The terrible conditions under which men, women and children laboured in the weaving factories in that town, together with the extreme poverty brought about by the agricultural depression of the time, ensured that that meeting led to immediate action. On Christmas Day of that year there was a demonstration at Caersws to the west, and in the following April a second meeting at Newtown. It was then that active discontent spread to Llanidloes, and riots started in the town on April 25th. Despite the presence of the police, the Chartists managed to get control of the town for three days from May 1st.

For once, the drovers going into England would have important political news to take with them. Their way led over the short ridgeway of the Kerry Hills, which has been claimed as the oldest road in Wales. To start that journey, go along the Newtown road until you reach the pretty village of Llandinam.

Map K page 145

Go through the village, keeping to the main road, and just before you reach the end of the speed limit you will see a lane on your right. Turn here, go left when it divides and then keep

044893 right until you reach a telephone box, where a sharp right-hand turn brings you to the farm of Little London – a name that always indicates an association with droving times. At this farm the lane ends and a track runs steeply up hill. Do not make for the summit of Moeliart, which stands on your right, but turn to your left for a little way, and then head due south for the

050878 wireless mast that dominates these hills. When you make the descent from the mast you will find a farm-track running to the east which brings you to the lane which connects the farms in

053873 the surrounding hills with the village of Mochdre. These lanes join to form a loop, and the village lies in the north-east corner. You come off the hill to the south-west, so that a turning in either direction will bring you to the village, although the route to your left is probably the more direct.

If you want to prolong the walk on the hills, don't take the track below the wireless mast, but carry on with the path that climbs the next hill to the south and brings you to the tumulus

044862 at the summit known as Giant's Grave – a common name to indicate a large prehistoric barrow. At this point turn east to descend by either of the hill paths running each side of a valley lying to the north-east. Both these paths will bring you out on farm tracks that lead to the Mochdre 'loop'. From that village you climb up on to the A road that runs between Newtown and Llandrindod Wells. Turn right along this road and stay with it till you come to a few buildings and a telephone box on a very

106870 sharp bend. This is the village of Dolfor.

Do not take the road that runs immediately to your left at Dolfor, but go just round the corner, where you will find another left-hand road that runs to Knighton. This road runs steeply up to the Kerry heights. Follow it until you come to the second of the farm buildings on your right to be made of black

108846 corrugated iron. This farm, known as Cider House, must have fulfilled exactly that function for the drovers, who met here for the last stretch of the journey into England.

There is a gate opposite this farm, but no public footpath sign. This is the start of the three-mile (4.8 kilometres) walk along

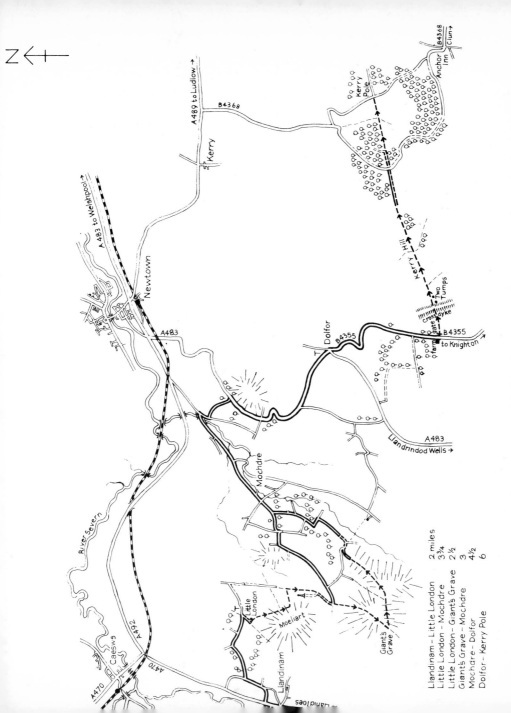

Map K

N

A489 to Ludlow →

B4368

Kerry

A483 to Welshpool →

Newtown

A483

River Severn

A492

Caersws

A470

A470

Llandinam

Handloes

Dolfor

B4355

Mochdre

Little London

Moeliart

Giant's Grave

Kerry Pole

B4368
Anchor Inn
Clun →

Kerry Dyke

Two Tumps
cross dyke
farm gate
B4355
to Knighton

A483
Llandrindod Wells →

Llandinam – Little London   2 miles
Little London – Mochdre   3¾
Little London – Giant's Grave   2½
Giant's Grave – Mochdre   3
Mochdre – Dolfor   4½
Dolfor – Kerry Pole   6

On the Kerry Ridgeway

the ridgeway of Kerry Hill, a track that was old to Stone Age man, and well trodden before ever it was used as a cattle way. A few hundred yards from the gate you will find that the way is crossed by the straight line of the ditch. This is all that is left of the fortifications that once guarded this hilltop settlement. Just past the earthworks the track runs close by twin barrows, known locally and marked on maps as the Two Tumps. This must have made an ancient sighting point. It was also the best-known gathering point for the Monmouthshire cattle.

From here the track runs almost directly north-east along the
164866 ridgeway to join the road at the bleak farm of Kerry Pole. You
can either take the lane that runs directly east and into
England over the hilltop ways until you drop down to Bishops
Castle, which is the way the cattle would have been taken, or
you can turn down hill to your right, through the hamlet of
Anchor and so on to Clun.

Alternatively, you can turn left and make your way down into
the valley of the Mule, and the town of Kerry itself, which is
some four miles (6.4 kilometres) from the ridgeway. Another
four miles brings you to Newtown where you can take a train.
147901 Kerry church is worth a visit on the way. It is kept open, and
although it initially strikes you as an ordinary Victorian
reconstruction, you can still find many traces of its medieval
past, including the fourteenth-century nave roof. When the
original church on this site was consecrated in 1176, Giraldus
Cambrensis, the first Welsh travel writer, was Archdeacon of
Brecon. He was so furious to think that the new church might
be handed over to the Bishop of St Asaph that he hurried to the
spot to defend his rights. He won his claim, but not before
threats of excommunication and clods of earth had been hurled
at the clerics of the northern diocese.

The Way to Hereford

This route starts in the stretch of high, wild land that lies to the east of the Teifi, as it flows between Tregaron and Lampeter. This is the Welsh desert, fourteen miles (22.5 kilometres) across from Tregaron to Abergwesyn, and one of the most renowned of the drove ways. This large area of desolate country is not a designated national park or conservation area, although it is quite as bleak and wild, and in many ways as impressive as the granite rocks of Snowdonia or the red sandstone heights of the Brecon Beacons. Much of it still belongs to the Birmingham Water Corporation, and farmsteads that the drovers knew lie beneath the midlands water supply.

This section of the book divides into four routes. The three northern ones start the eastern part of the journey when they cross the Wye at Rhayader, Newbridge and Builth Wells respectively. Once across that river, the way goes over the Radnorshire hills and the tracks become less lonely. But although the hills are gentler here, this is still wild country with waterfalls, deciduous woodlands and the best wild raspberries I have ever found.

The southern route crosses the Teifi above Lampeter, goes through the Cothi valley to the north of Pumpsaint, over a high plateau on which traces of hut circles dating from the Bronze Age have been found, and down to the steep valley of the Tywi. There we have to abandon the route and take it up again a few miles to the west of Erwood, north of Brecon. The area in between is the vast high plateau of Mynydd Eppynt (the mountain of the horses) which is now a military zone and only intermittently safe for walkers.

The three northern routes cross into England through Knighton, and they converge on that section of Offa's Dyke which follows the Hergest Ridge. To the south the way to Hereford lies across the Painscastle and Clyro hills to meet the A438 at Rhydspence.

Aberystwyth/Rhayader

(Ordnance Survey sheet 147)

Disused quarry near Bodtalog

It is still possible to get a train to Aberystwyth, and that's a good way to go if you intend following the drove routes as they run east through mid-Wales. Alternatively, you can make good circular walks along the drove ways in both this and the preceding section by basing yourself at the Youth Hostel of Tanrallt near Llangurig.

In any case, Aberystwyth is an interesting town to visit. This university/seaside place still holds many memories of the drovers. If you turn left when you come out of the station, and then take the second turning on your left, along the road to which traffic for the south is directed, you will see about fifty yards (45.7 metres) on your left the large red doors of Brian Lewis's Cambrian forge. His father, Emlyn Lewis, believes that he is the last blacksmith still working at his trade to have shod oxen. He did it in the mid-1920s when Atora beef suet ran an advertising stunt, touring the country with a caravan drawn by two oxen weighing about eighteen hundredweight each. They stayed in Aberystwyth for three days, and on the second day the oxen were brought to the forge. Mr Lewis, who was about twenty at the time, recalls that they were 'pure bred Hereford, and gave very little trouble to shoe'.

Your way lies south, but before you leave the city it's worthwhile turning right into Bridge Street. There you will see the old Bank Inn on your right. Across the road from it is a terrace house with a stone sheep embossed on the wall. This is now a students' hostel, but it was once a very important drovers' bank. The Banc-y-Ddafad was started in 1762, and it issued its own bank notes until the end of the last century, by

151

which time it was amalgamated with a Tregaron bank and run by Evans, Jones, Davies & Co. You can see one of these bank notes in the market-place museum at Llanidloes. The one on display there has two sheep on it, signifying that the banknote was worth £2. A ten-shilling note would have had a black lamb on it. No note was made out for a sum greater than £5. This pictorial method was designed for the benefit of the drovers who could not read or understand numerical symbols.

742771   From Aberystwyth you will have to make your way south-east to Devil's Bridge along the A4120 either by bus or car. This was an important centre for the cattle and boasted a shoeing station, whose products were once used in a fairly cunning trick. It is an eighteenth-century story of set-a-thief-to-catch-a-thief. A sailor, who had run away from a foreign ship that was smuggling brandy into the Cardiganshire ports, went along with the droves to London. It was a case of mutual protection. When this particular drove was held up in the wild country to the east of Devil's Bridge, the leader of the drovers gave the sailor a money bag filled with clinking ox cues to give to the highway-man, who seems to have been easily persuaded that the bag contained sovereigns. When he galloped off with this false loot, the sailor killed him with his catapult. Today's tourist needs to be almost as wary as that highwayman in these parts. Some-how, when you have to pay to go through a hideous metal turnstile to look at a natural phenomenon, even the beautiful waterfalls of the Rheidol lose their magic.

From Devil's Bridge three choices present themselves. You can either take the north-easterly route to Llangurig; you can go south to Ffair Rhos and then directly east to Rhayader; or you can go further south as far as Strata Florida and then continue south over the mountains to join the route from Tregaron to Abergwesyn.

The first choice runs through wild and interesting country, but the track has now been made into a road. However, it is still pleasant enough to walk along, until the work on the new reservoir gets under way. From Devil's Bridge follow the B4574 to Cwmystwyth. This leads you to the mountain road for Rhayader, and the disused lead mines with the bleak barracks which were once home to the young men from the farms who

823753   came to work here. Past the mines you come to Tyllwyd, which was once a drovers' inn.

827756   Just past Tyllwyd you will see a track going into the mountains past the farm of Blaenycwm. This track goes through two stretches of forest land, and comes out by some farm buildings to
895802   join the A44 just above Llangurig. From there you can either go south to Rhayader, head straight for Abbeycwmhir along the route which is outlined on page 166 or go to the Youth Hostel, by

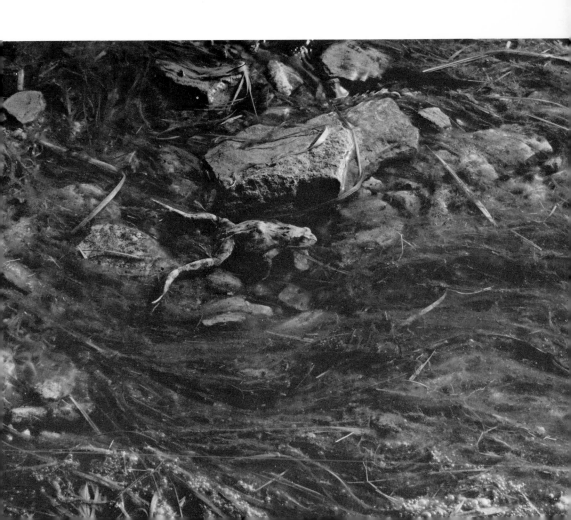

following the lane that runs due south past Llangurig church and along the west bank of the Wye for about four miles (6.4 kilometres), until you reach a sign on your right directing you to the hostel.

867746   If you carry on towards Rhayader along the mountain road, instead of turning to your left at Blaenycwm, you will find after you have gone about three miles (4.8 kilometres) that there is a track running up the mountainside to the farm of Bodtalog. At least you could find it in 1976, and I hope you will still be able for a year or so yet. It depends how long it takes for the plans for the new reservoir, which is designed to flood this narrow valley, to be put into effect. When that scheme goes ahead Mr William Pugh, who farms Bodtalog now, and his neighbours across the valley at Abergwngu Hill, will have to leave the mountain farms which their families have tended for generations – and the tourists will crowd the road in their cars to see the new dams.

This seems to be an ill-fated place, for it was here, too, that one of the saddest incidents of the nineteenth-century Rebecca Riots took place. These riots were methodical attacks on the toll gates which were put up by landowners and private companies licensed to undertake road improvement schemes. Although it was necessary that the roads should be improved, to keep Wales up with nineteenth-century progress, the heavy toll charges made the public highway too expensive for working men. George Borrow's guide in Llangollen, John Jones, explained what happened:

Ruins of old Claerwen Farm

Some say that there were a hundred Rebeccas and all of them dressed in women's clothes, who went about at night at the heads of bands to break the gates. Ah, sir, something of the kind was almost necessary at that time. I am a friend of peace, sir; no head-breaker, house-breaker, nor gate-breaker, but I can hardly blame what was done at that time, under the name of Rebecca. You have no idea how the poor Welsh were oppressed by those gates, aye, and the rich too. The little people and farmers could not carry their produce to market owing to the exactions at the gates, which devoured all the profit and sometimes more ... Complaints were made to government, which not being attended to, Rebecca and her hyddinion made their appearance at night, and broke the gates to pieces with sledge-hammers, and everybody said it was gallant work, everybody save the keepers of the gates and the proprietors. [5]

The irony was that the proprietors suffered far less from these acts of violence than their underpaid servants who kept the gates. It was a solitary old woman who kept the toll among the lonely crags at Bodtalog. The historian David Williams recounts what happened to her on the night of October 9th, 1843: 'A rioter fired his powder-load gun in her face and injured both her eyes. She had recognised her assailants, but later denied all knowledge of them and "acted like a raving lunatic" through fear of reprisals. The authorities offered the usual reward of £50 for information.' [6] But it was not forthcoming, and by the end of the month another gate in the Rhayader area was attacked.

The drovers who were going this way would have had other matters beside toll gates to worry about. For many of them contracted with the gold miners who scratched a little of the precious metal out of these rocks to carry the gold to the bullion dealers of London and share the proceeds on a fifty-fifty basis. So they may well have found it safer to stay on the old Aberystwyth road to Rhayader, rather than try any short-cuts over the mountains.

However, that need not stop you from taking the mountain path past Bodtalog and following it along the valley, to climb the slopes of Esgair Ganol and cross the mountain pass for Pont-gwyn Hill, from where you can descend to the Wye and the lane that leads to the Youth Hostel.

739680 The second main choice of route from Devil's Bridge takes you south along the B4343 through Pontrhydygroes and Ysbyty Ystwyth to Ffair Rhos, which was once a big centre for cattle markets. Now follow the mountain road due east, until just above Llyn Teifi you see a single large stone. This is not of prehistoric significance, but was once part of a pair of stones in between which a bullock could be wedged for shoeing.

As the track goes east into the mountains it becomes much less well-defined, for here the animals would have been allowed to

155

Pen-y-garreg Reservoir

spread out to pick up what grazing they could. Head east across rough hilly country for a mile (1.6 kilometres) until you come to a place where you can ford the Claerddu. If you follow this river to the south-east you will find that it runs into the head of the Claerwen Reservoir.

805677

You can go more directly east, however, by crossing Esgair Hengae and then picking up the ancient track to the east of the Claerwen. This climbs steeply towards the crags beside Llyn Cerrigllwydion Uchaf and then runs along the ridgeway for about five miles (eight kilometres), until it descends towards the road at the motor bridge across the Elan River and the road leading to the reservoir created by the City of Birmingham in the early years of this century. All the land in these parts has belonged to Birmingham Corporation since the 1890s, and in those years it was possible to get a farm for an annual rent of £5.

824682

903716

For a fictional account of the flooding, read Francis Brett Young's *The House Under the Water*.[7] The house he probably had in mind was the one in which Shelley came to live in 1812. It was called Nantgwyllt, and as a newly married man of nineteen Shelley found it a place where nature was marked with 'the most impressive character of loveliness and grandeur'. Recalling how apparently insensitive he was to the draining of the Porthmadog marshes, it is interesting to wonder what his reaction would have been to the modern dam, and the waters which covered this valley until the disastrously dry summers of 1975 and 1976 revealed long-drowned farms.

From the Elan Bridge you can take the road along the western side of the Craig Goch Reservoir. Cross the dam at its southern end and take the track going east over Esgair-perfedd to meet the road to Rhayader. The alternative is to cross the water at the northern end by the Elan Bridge and then head south for Rhayader. Whichever way you get on to this road, you will want to leave it by the tracks that run east at 916715 or at 922707. The first of these tracks runs along the north side of a valley, crosses the stream of Nant y Sarn and then climbs steeply to the rocks of Llofftyddgleision, from where it makes an equally steep descent to the lane on the western side of the Wye.

893687

Dam at Pen-y-garreg Reservoir

This is a very ancient track, but as it is so steep and runs so close to dangerous precipices it is more likely that the herds would have followed the more southerly of the two routes. When this track leaves the mountain road, it runs for some time almost parallel to it. Yet even here, despite the holiday traffic on the scenic route of the old road, this great stretch of marshy hill country which makes up the desert of Wales still exercises its extraordinary lonely power. That is probably why, even on clear sunny days, so few tourists can bring themselves to leave their cars. For which one may be thankful.

The old track, which shows traces of its original paving, skirts the side of a hill and eventually brings you out to a small eminence surmounted by a standing stone, which aeons ago someone put up to mark this track. The stone reminded me of

Daniel Defoe's attempts to explain the stone circles and the standing stones which he encountered during his tour of Wales:

Nor is it doubted that they were generally monuments of the dead, as also are the single stones of immense bulk ... of which we saw so many that we gave over remarking them, some we saw from seven, eight, ten and one sixteen foot long, being a whole stone, but so great that most of the wonder is, where they were found, and how dragg'd to the place, since besides the steep ascents to some of the hills on which they stand, it would be impossible to move some of them now with fifty yokes of oxen.

At the stone the track divides. If you take the left-hand path you will descend steeply to the Wye at Cwmcoch, where you can either cross the river to join the main Aberystwyth road or turn right for Rhayader. The right-hand path takes a more gentle descent to the south-east, and rejoins the Rhayader road just above a cattle grid.

742680

The third route from Devil's Bridge takes you south to Strata Florida. To reach the ruins of this abbey from Ffair Rhos, you can either take the road through Pontrhydfendigaid or leave the village by the lane running south-east across the mountains. This track takes you to the west of Esgair y Garn and through a stretch of woodland, from where it descends to the Teifi valley. You come out on to a lane a little way to the east of the ruins. At Strata Florida, the medieval poet Dafydd ap Gwilym lies buried. If Twm o'r Nant was the Welsh Shakespeare, here is the Welsh Chaucer. Nigel Heseltine has translated twenty-five of these fourteenth-century poems, all of which in one way or another deal with the poet's love for an inaccessible lady – usually either a nun or a married woman in the best courtly tradition. Once, however, he deserted this high ideal for a girl he picked up at an inn, only to be similarly frustrated. For when he tried to get into her bed he 'came upon a damned obstruction in the shape of three Englishmen in one stinking bed, pedlars with three packs lying around ... Hicken and Shockin and Shack or some such names'. The translations were published by the Piers Press, Banbury in 1968.

The cattle would probably have been driven from Strata Florida along the Teifi, which you follow until it joins the

Standing stone, Maen-serth

Mwyro. From its source the route goes south by the west bank
of Llyn Gorast towards the Towy Forest. Turn left along the
edge of the forest by the stream of Nant Gwineu. This stream
goes directly south down a valley to the farm of Nant-ystalwyn,
which is now a holiday cottage. From there it is a few yards to
the Tregaron/Abergwesyn road.

792631

805576

The Youth Hostel of Dolgoch is about a mile and a half (2.4
kilometres) to the south of this road. The walks and drove paths
in this area are given on pages 181-90.

810565

To take up the story again at Rhayader. In her documentary
novel *The Valley*, the novelist Elizabeth Clarke, who lives just
outside the town, tells how the droves left that centre:

Strata Florida Abbey

*At a forge where the geese were shod cattle were fitted with
shoes, before making their way across England with drovers
who carried extra pairs for replacement, and a supply of nails
embedded in a lump of fat bacon to keep them from rusting. All
the young men lent a hand in starting the droves on their way,
and some made the whole journey. These beasts were wild when
they came off the hills, and in the first place they had to be
urged through the Wye to avoid the toll gate on the road out of
Rhayader.*

In Radnorshire generally the usual eighteenth-century toll was
10d for a score of cattle; but it was possible to avoid the
Rhayader gate by crossing south of the town by the Triangle
Inn and coming out on to the Nantmor road, and so continuing
the journey east.

Rhayader, which is now a fairly prosperous little market town,
doing quite well out of the tourists who are drawn mainly by
the Elan and Claerwen reservoirs, presented a different picture
a hundred years ago. Then, according to the historian David
Williams, it was 'a town of wretched mud hovels, invariably
fronted with a pig-sty or dunghill or both. It was the only town
in Radnorshire where Welsh was spoken and it was the market
centre for an extensive and wild countryside.' It has always been
an important road junction for farmers, being the natural place
to which stock would be brought from the farms on the
Plynlimon range to the north, for it lies conveniently on the

way going east into England.

Each of the six gates into the town was marked with a toll gate, so that when the Rebecca Riots hit Rhayader in September 1843 the men had a lot to work on, and a host of long-smouldering grievances to stimulate them. David Williams describes the first attack thus: 'The first outbreak occurred on Monday night, September 25th at the Llangurig end of the new road from Rhayader which now formed part of the route from Cheltenham to Aberystwyth. On Thursday night two gates, placed where a lane branched off from the old Aberystwyth road beyond the bridge over the Wye at Rhayader, were pulled down with all the pomp and paraphernalia of Rebecca.'[10] In October came the attack on the Bodtalog toll. Then, after attacking the gate at Newbridge-on-Wye to the south, within the course of a month Rebecca turned her attention with renewed fury to Rhayader.

On the night of November 2nd about 150 rioters entered the town in three contingents. David Williams tells how 'they met at the St Harmon gate, demolished it then proceeded to the other gates. In all they destroyed four gates and a toll house.'[11]

In the new year the Llangurig gate was destroyed, on May 3rd Rebecca attacked the Llanidloes gate, and the attacks went on intermittently until mid-September. Perhaps it was at this time that, as Elizabeth Clarke recalls, a circus elephant was employed to push down a gate at the owner's command.

Yet although the toll-gate system in Wales was often run with great injustice, was always partly a way of making the rich richer, and was a cause of great bitterness in counties whose largest landowners were Englishmen who never set foot in Wales, something certainly had to be done if the roads were to be kept passable at all. Radnorshire's historian, W. H. Howse, describes the state of the thoroughfares in the seventeenth and eighteenth centuries thus: 'There was practically no wheeled traffic, and goods were conveyed by panniered horses or donkeys, or on sledges drawn by horses or oxen. Where waggons were employed there are records of as many as sixteen horses being required to drag them through the mud. There are also records of people being drowned in the roads.'[12]

928738

Map L page 167
The most interesting way east from Rhayader starts at Dolhelfa on the Llangurig road. If you are going to make this walk from the Tanrallt hostel, you will find that the lane running by the Wye to the south soon crosses the river and joins the A470 just opposite the Dolhelfa path.

This is the start of the hill track for Abbeycwmhir. These hills to the east of Rhayader are far less wild and desolate than the ones that lie in the wasteland to the west. But they are so beautiful that Bernard Shaw declared, 'No man ought to be in the government of this land who does not spend three months of every year in country such as this.'

The hills are full of drovers' tracks, although as W.H. Howse explains they are not always easy to trace because, 'starting from many different points and with a variety of destinations their routes are naturally widespread. There are few hills in the eastern parts of the county which the drovers did not use.'[13] The tracks that they used in the country around St Harmon and Abbeycwmhir were no doubt those along which Owen Glendower brought his men in the first months of the fifteenth century, as he came out of his Plynlimon fastness to drive the English settlers out of Wales.

938747

967723
The clear track from Dolhelfa climbs for about a mile and a half (2.4 kilometres) to a shooting box on the banks of Marcheini Fawr. From that point, you can either turn south-east and follow the course of the stream past a waterfall and through overhanging crags on to the lane three miles (4.8 kilometres) to the west of St Harmon, or you can carry on across the mountains to the north-east. That way will bring you eventually to a field gate leading to a grassy track running beside a new forestry plantation. The trees which stand on your right are only some three years old as yet, and so for a year or two they will not much obstruct the landscape.

952767
At the bottom of the hill the grassy track becomes a farm lane, bears to the right and runs through the farmyard of Craig-gellidywyll. Before you get to the farm, leave the track by the gate on your left. Here the lane runs around a valley, past a new house and a single standing stone of some size. Follow this lane as it goes east, having re-crossed the Dulas, and leave it when

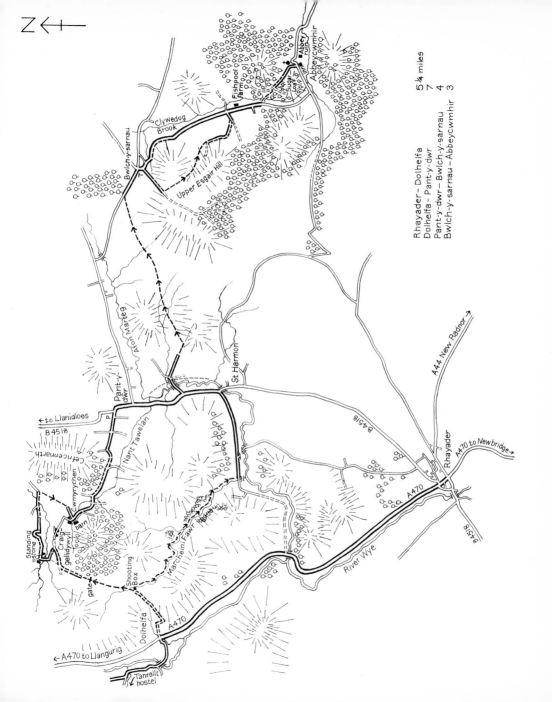

N←↑

Rhayader – Dolhelfa   5¼ miles
Dolhelfa – Pant-y-dwr   7
Pant-y-dwr – Bwlch-y-sarnau   4
Bwlch-y-sarnau – Abbeycwmhir   3

Abbeycwmhir
Abbey ruins
Sugar Loaf
Fishpool Farm
Clywedog Brook
Bwlch-y-sarnau
Upper Esgair Hill
Afon Marteg
Pant-y-dwr
St Harmon
A44 New Radnor
←to Llanidloes
B4518
Cefncennarth
Cwmyrychen
Craig gellidywyll
barn
Nant Tawelan
Marcheini Fawr
Shooting Box
Standing stone
gate
B4518
A4518
Rhayader
A470 to Newbridge→
A470
River Wye
Dolhelfa
A470
←A470 to Llangurig
Tanrallt hostel

964771   you see a path on your right. This eventually merges into a hollow lane which brings you out a little to the south-east of Craig-gellidywyll. You are now standing opposite the old barn of

957763   Cwmyrychen Farm. This is one of the oldest cruck buildings in mid-Wales, and one of the support beams has been roughly chamfered, an indication of the early importance of the building. The barn was included in the deal when the farmer here sold his acres to the Forestry Commission, but fortunately it has been reprieved and is now being patiently restored as a dwelling house.

From Cwmyrychen the way goes south-east, past the lovely deciduous wood of Cefncennarth and to the road by the post office of Pant-y-dŵr. From here the road goes south towards St

987736   Harmon. After about a mile and a half (2.4 kilometres), you will come to a track on your left, which crosses the river. Take the right-hand fork over the old railway track, and then follow the path which goes along the northern slopes of the hill. This 023750 path, which soon turns north-east, runs across open country for some three miles (4.8 kilometres) and brings you out just above the village of Bwlch-y-sarnau.

From there you can either follow the lanes to Abbeycwmhir, or you can take the track on your right opposite the church. This climbs steeply towards the forestry land, but before you reach the trees it is crossed by the ridgeway path running across 036729 Upper Esgair Hill. This comes out on a farm track which you follow down the hill to the road just above Fishpool Farm, whose name commemorates the first monastic fish ponds in Britain. Turn right and go past the farm along the road for about half a mile (804 metres), until you see the very overgrown 045719 entrance to a green lane on your left. This was once a paved causeway.

Standing stones near Cwmyrychen Farm

After a scramble through the undergrowth you come to a stream crossed by a rotting plank bridge. If you don't feel like risking the bridge, which stands about four feet (1.2 metres) above the stream, you can easily ford it. The track now gets much clearer and runs through Forestry Commission land. Follow it to the north of the little Sugar Loaf hill, crossing the forestry lane twice as you do so. As the track descends towards the village of Abbeycwmhir, you will find that for a little way you are walking along the remains of an old narrow gauge railway. This takes you to a gate, and from here the path runs along the side of a stream to emerge to the west of Abbeycwm-hir church and opposite the oddly named 'Happy Union' Inn. You must not leave this village without walking round the remains of the abbey, which is the burial place of Llewelyn ap Gruffudd, last native Prince of Wales, who was killed near Builth Wells in December 1282. The ruins are not immediately easy to find. Leave the church by the road running east towards Crossgates, as the drovers would have done, and just as you start to climb the hill out of the village you will see a gate on your right. This is the entrance to the field where the ruins are, its few crumbling walls now serving as sheep shelters.

The abbey, which was founded at the end of the twelfth

Abbeycwmhir

century, was virtually destroyed during the expeditions of Owen Glendower, and although it was in use to the time of the Reformation only three monks were found to be in it when it was finally dissolved in 1536. R. C. B. Oliver, in a paper on 'The Shelleys and Radnorshire',[14] quotes a rhyme originally supposed to date from Cromwell's time, which shows that the abbey lands had made a rich living for the landowners:

In Radnorshire is neither knight nor peer
Nor park with deer, nor gentlemen with 500 a year
Except Sir William Fowler of Abbey Cwmhir.

This Sir William, whose father Richard was sheriff of the county in 1655, built the village church out of the stones of the old abbey. That was demolished in its turn, and the present neo-Gothic building was put up in 1865.

From the village of the abbey, take the lane running south by the banks of the Clywedog Brook. When the lane meets the main road turn right to Crossgates and then left to Penybont. From there you can get a train going east into England, or south-west towards Llandovery. If you have time for more walks in this area, you could take a train along that west-bound track as far as Builth Road, and then follow the route outlined on page 181.

099648

Newbridge to Kington

(Ordnance Survey sheets 147/148)

The most famous of all the Welsh drove routes runs for fourteen miles (22.5 kilometres) across the wide moorland, known as the desert of Wales, which stretches between Tregaron and Abergwesyn. The mountain road is made up now, but you will find the walks that lie to the north and south of it in the sections based on Aberystwyth (pages 151-70) and Llandovery (pages 191-222). This section follows the herds east from Abergwesyn.

Map M page 173 To get to Abergwesyn, catch the train to Llanwrtyd-Wells and then take the minor road which runs northwards to the village along the banks of the Irfon. This road was once travelled in the opposite direction by the first cattle and sheep to make the journey to England by rail. They came from the mountains to Abergwesyn and were then taken by train from Llanwrtyd to Reading. One of the first drovers to make this journey with the beasts was William Probert, remembered as Billy Boy, who accompanied a flock of mountain ewes.

Before the railways, the route lay eastwards from Abergwesyn to Beulah. The droves would not have taken the present road t that village. They went the shorter way, which leaves the river and runs straight across the hills. This track is still locally known as the Cefn Cardis (the Cardiganshire Path). There is a right of way dispute going on at present over this path, which is fenced across half-way up the hillside. The track is still very clear, however, and you can follow it for a little way by taking the lane that runs south from Abergwesyn just opposite the Grouse Inn and the turning for the mountain road to Tregaron.

855527   This path fords a stream, and then starts to climb very gently up the side of the hill to the left. Near the hilltop the way is blocked by the fence. You can see the track though, running on across the Cefn Waun-lwyd. If you were able to follow it, it would take you through a narrow belt of forest and then to a farm track, which comes out on the road just north of Beulah.

As things are, you must either go all the way by the lane to Beulah, a matter of six miles (9.6 kilometres), or rejoin the Cefn Cardis by crossing the River Cnyffiad at 893527. The path climbs through the forest to the south-east, and when you emerge from the trees you will find that your way is crossed by the old drove track. Turn left and follow it through towards the farm of Aber-Annell. When the track divides turn left again, and you will come out on to the lane about half a mile (804 metres) to the west of Beulah.

916515

0158 To reach Newbridge, the next drove centre to the east, take the B road through Beulah village. This crosses the Cammarch and runs north-east past the church. The eight-mile (12.8 kilometres) stretch of road you have now embarked on has the hamlet of Llanafan-fawr as a half-way mark. It is worth stopping at for its Red Lion Inn, which must surely be the smallest pub in Britain. It is simply a room in a farm house, and one of the best examples of the kind of place where the drovers would expect to find refreshment.

To get into Newbridge you cross the Wye by an unprepossessing modern bridge. On its south side you can see the ford, which is how the cattle got across. On the east bank you'll find the drove track very clearly marked, going up from the river bank and under a disused railway bridge, after which it turns into a lane running beside the church.

If you stay on the road to the east of the bridge you will shortly come to the Mid-Wales Art Gallery. It was known to the drovers as the Mid-Wales Inn, and a great meeting place it was. It is now run by Nancy Palmer-Jones, who organizes exhibitions of work by Welsh artists, and whose own particular interest is in natural dyes made out of plants in the neighbourhood. The vegetable colours that she uses date from medieval times.

When you reach the main road running through the village,

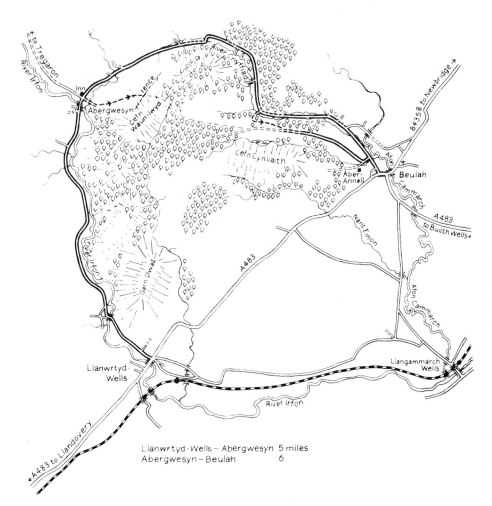

N

Llanwrtyd-Wells – Abergwesyn 5 miles
Abergwesyn – Beulah   6

turn right towards Builth Wells until you come to the village
school on your left. The lane which runs beside the school

024582 brings you to Woodcastle Farm. This is no longer inhabited,
although the farm buildings are still in use. The way goes
through the farmyard, across a very muddy track and through a
field. You are now climbing the slopes of a small hill.

At the top of this hill there is a gateway, and the track divides.
The clearest track runs to the right round the side of the hill
and enters a small wood. Ignore it and take the fainter path.
This runs down the hill to join a few yards of old green lane,
clearly banked on either side. When this fragment comes to an
end, take the stile on your left and climb up a field path, which
brings you to the spinney that overlooks the River Ithon as it
bends round Disserth church.

The old drove route would naturally have gone along a
continuation of the green lane, and not along the present path.
You will soon realize that it would not have been easy to drive
cattle down the short, steep slope of that hill. When you reach
the bottom of the hill, turn diagonally to the left across a field
until you find the gate in the hedge that leads on to the road.
Here you turn right for Howey and Crossway.

035585 Just after you have crossed the road bridge you will notice a
lane on your right leading to Disserth church. Despite the
caravan site which now stands on the banks of the river, in the
fields belonging to the farm which was once a drovers' inn, the
church is worth visiting. Like many small Welsh churches its
attraction from the outside lies in its extreme simplicity, which
in this case is not any preparation for the surprise of its interior.
This is one of the very few places, if not the only one, where the
seventeenth-century wooden pews are all retained and completely fill the body of the church. Among them stands the old
three-decker pulpit. W. H. Howse has written about the history
of this church and the people who willingly or not came here
Sunday by Sunday.[15] For the rich families it cannot have been
too bad. They expected their servants to bring tea to their pews,
and no one took exception to the occasional game of cards being
played when the sermon got tedious.

When you leave the church to carry on the journey towards

Crossway, you have two alternative routes to choose from. When the lane meets the main road (A483) running between Llandrindod Wells and Builth Wells, you can either turn left for Howey or you can carry on the journey to the east by taking the minor road ahead of you, sign-posted to Hundred House.

If you decide to visit Howey, which was a great meeting place for the drovers, you will find that the old drovers' inn there is now run as a small, lively hotel, from which you can hire bikes

050583

Disserth church

to follow some of the drove routes that run along the lanes in
this region. Howey, which now is a cluster of houses beside the
main road, was once a sizeable town, and the drovers would
have known it as a much larger place than Llandrindod Wells.
That town owes its size and prosperity purely to the Victorians'
faith in the healing powers of mineral waters.

Should you have decided to go straight on towards Hundred
House, you will be following the route along which geese and
turkeys as well as cattle were driven. Today's road crosses a
cattle grid and then becomes a good mountain road, which it is
086567   pleasant to walk along. When it takes you through a pass with
Gilwern Hill on your left, take the right-hand fork towards
Llansantffraed-in-Elvel. Before you reach that tiny village, you
096557   can take the second farm track on your left. This crosses a

stream, and once it has passed the farm buildings becomes a footpath running to the east of Hirllwyn Bank. This runs through scattered woodlands to join the track to Frank's Bridge. (If you decide to take a look at Llansantffraed, you will find that this track enters the village just behind the telephone box.)

107553
099547

You come out just below Frank's Bridge, which you reach by turning left and then almost immediately right. A footpath just opposite the church brings you to the main road (A481) between Builth Wells and New Radnor. Immediately opposite you there is a footpath sign which directs you across a field to Pen-rhiw Farm. From there follow the farm track until you meet a lane. Turn left, away from the road, and climb with the track to the tumulus known as Giant's Grave. This is one of the most outstanding of the hilltop barrows. No one knows who was buried here, but the mound was clearly intended to serve the additional function of marking the way across the mountains. This area had many scattered settlements in prehistoric times. Perhaps the man, or more likely the people, who lay beneath this hilltop worshipped at the solid, dark-green rock which has now become the font of Old Radnor church to the north-east. This is one of the few open churches, so you can always have a look at it. The rock is believed to have been a pre-Christian altar. It was hollowed out by Celtic priests and it has been used for baptisms since the sixth century.

117561

119552

140544

rch carving, Disserth church

From Giant's Grave the way goes downhill. Take the left-hand path when the tracks divide, and then cross another farm lane to the bridge which crosses the stream below Glascwm village. When you reach the village you will be immediately confronted by the Youth Hostel, which is housed in the old school.

158533

There was a drovers' inn in Glascwm village up to 1913, although by that date the drovers who took food and shelter there would have been on comparatively short journeys. Sir Rhys Rankin, who has made a study of the farming history of mid-Wales, reckons that it was in 1900 that the last drove of mountain ewes from Tregaron would have come this way, to go on through Colva and Gladestry on their way to Harrow-on-the-Hill. If you decide to take that road to the east, you will find the route from Gladestry to Kington outlined in the next section.

The alternative open to you from Glascwm is to go north to join the drove route from Frank's Bridge to Dolyhir. If you decide to do this, go back to the stream at the north of the village; immediately after you have crossed the bridge, take the path on your right. This runs to the west of Gwaunceste Hill, and then turns due north to join a farm track. Follow it through to the north-west, until it joins the A481. Turn right here and go along the main road for a couple of miles. Just before you get to Forest Inn, you will see a hill track on your right running to the north of a small pool, Llynheilyn. The track now runs due east towards Pentre Tump. Take the track that runs round the south side of this mound and then north-east towards the farm of Wolfpits (whose name is a reminder that the last wolves in Britain roamed this area in the seventeenth century).

155554
147575

167584
195578

218588

When this farm track meets a lane, turn right to the village of Yardro, and go along the road that leads past the quarries of Dolyhir. From this village turn left along the road that runs through Burlingjobb, where you join the main road to Kington. If you make this part of the journey on a Tuesday, you may find that you are sharing the road with the sheep being brought into the weekly market at that town.

223588
246580

Builth Wells Market

Builth Wells to Kington

(Ordnance Survey sheets 147/148)

Map N page 183

Instead of going north-east to Newbridge, some of the herds which collected at Beulah would have been driven towards Builth Wells along the road which runs through Garth and Cilmery. A railway still runs along this way, and the best plan would be to take the train to Builth Road (the next stop, to the north-east, after Cilmery and about two miles [3.2 kilometres] north of the Wye from Builth Wells). From the station turn towards the town (that is to your right) but do not cross the bridge into it. From the great roundabout which now stands between the north side of that bridge and the permanent grounds of the Royal Welsh Show, take the main road towards New Radnor. Once you have passed the quarries of Llanelwedd on your left, you will see a B road on your right which runs along the eastern bank of the Wye. The herds would probably have been driven direct from Cilmery to Builth Wells along what is now the A483; then, in order to avoid paying tolls, the drovers could have taken them across the ford, at the point where the present minor road is separated from the river by a narrow spinney and an old railway track.

025534

062517

As you walk south along this road you will see several tracks running up to Aberedw Hill. Probably the best one to take starts from 068502. This brings you on to the ridge of the hill at a point slightly to the north of a tumulus which aligns with a pair of tumuli to the north-east. A track marks the way right along the ridge of the hill, whose land provides common grazing for the sheep and horses of the farmers of Hundred House. As you follow this track to the north-east, you will see on your left a surprising triangular-shaped green field. The surprise is the luxuriant grass here, which is particularly astonishing in a

079496

summer like that of 1976, when the rest of the hill was so bare that the animals had to have their grazing supplemented. This one patch owes much of its fertility to long-dead cattle, who over many years were pastured here for the night. For this is the site of an old drovers' inn, whose stones have long since been used for other buildings. The place is still known locally as Tabor Wye. It is likely that this was one of the inns that the drovers regularly used on their journey home. On the way back into Wales they usually joined up in twos and threes and travelled the same way as they had come. The only differences from the outward journey were that without the cattle it wasn't so essential to avoid the toll gates, and advantage could be taken of some short, steep ways, which even the nimble Welsh blacks couldn't manage.

By the side of the old pasture here, you will see the Scots pines which were planted to let the drovers know that the place offered refreshment. Some people will tell you a more romantic story about these trees. Popular tradition has it that they were planted in Cromwell's time as a sign of loyalty to the House of Stuart.

From Tabor Wye the sheep and cattle would have been driven south-east to Painscastle or north-east towards Glascwm. If you are based in this area, perhaps staying for two or three nights at the Glascwm Youth Hostel, you will find that you can combine these routes into several good, round walks.

The herds that were taken to Painscastle would have been driven first to the shoeing station of Cregrina. In the seventeenth century the last wolf to be shot in Wales met its end here. In Tudor times wolves frequently roamed these hills, and presented yet another danger to drovers, who had also to be constantly on the alert for attacks from brigands.

Builth Wells Old Market

116538

The most direct way to reach Cregrina from Tabor Wye is to follow the track going directly north-east. This brings you down from Aberedw Hill to the lane known as Hungry Green. Turn right along it, and when it forks, keep to the right-hand way. You pass a shapely castle mound on your right. This now lies in private land, but at one time it was known as a public meeting place. It was from here, in the mid-eighteenth century, that

182

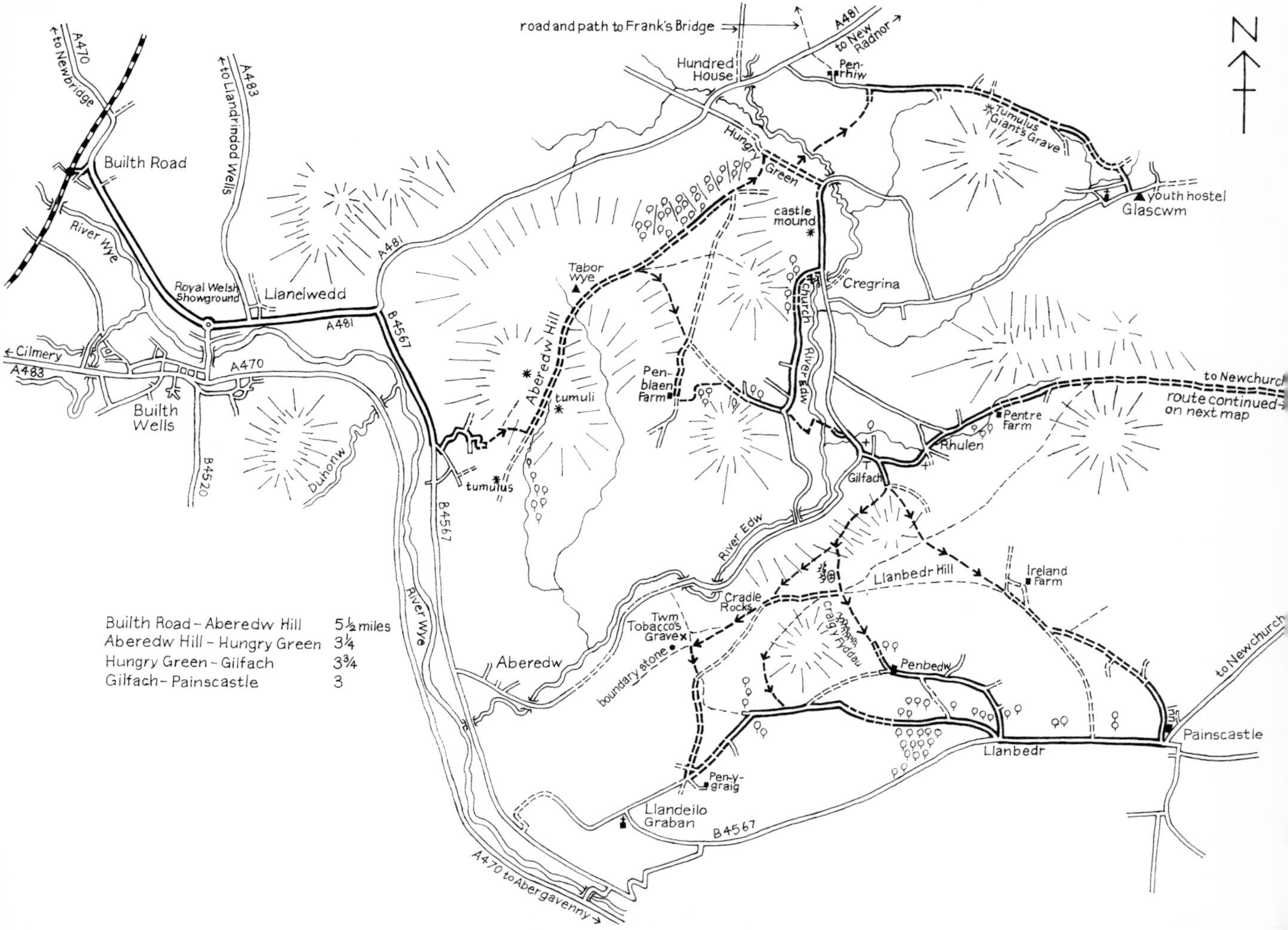

Map N

N

to Newchurch / route continued on next map

to Newchurch

Painscastle

youth hostel
Glascwm

Tumulus
Giant's Grave

Pentre Farm

Rhulen

Ireland Farm

Llanbedr

Penbedw

Llanbedr-Hill

Cregrina

Gilfach

Craig-y-Fyddau

Cradle Rocks

Pen-Rhiw

A481 to New Radnor

church

River Edw

castle mound

Hungry Green

Hundred House

road and path to Frank's Bridge

River Edw

Pen-y-graig

Llandeilo Graban

Pen-blaen Farm

Twm Tobacco's Grave

boundary stone

Tabor Wye

tumuli

Aberedw Hill

tumulus

Aberedw

B4567

B4567

A470 to Abergavenny

A481

River Wye

Llanelwedd

Buhona

A483
to Llandrindod Wells

A470

Royal Welsh Showground

B4520

Builth Road

Builth Wells

A470
to Newbridge

River Wye

Cilmery

A483

Builth Road – Aberedw Hill   5½ miles
Aberedw Hill – Hungry Green   3¾
Hungry Green – Gilfach   3¾
Gilfach – Painscastle   3

John Wesley preached one of his earliest outdoor sermons to the Welsh. He had an immediate following, for although he described the Welsh in his journals as being as pagan as any Red Indians, he made close friends among them, the greatest being the agriculturalist and evangelist Howell Harris of Trefecca. So Wesley was well known and loved in central Wales. When his brother Charles chose a Welsh bride, Sarah Gwynne of Garth, he married them in April 1749 at Llalleonfel church. As a result, however, before he spoke at Cregrina he lost the friendship of Edward Phillips, rector of Maesmynis church near Builth, who had travelled with him as far as Caernarvon to translate his sermons into Welsh, for he had wanted Sarah for his wife. Such personal considerations apart, Wesley's message spread like wild fire through Wales, fanned by the crushing poverty of so many people at that time and the indifference of the great (mainly English) landowners and the established Church.

124522   You are now a little way north of Cregrina village. Here your best way is to take the lane on your right, which climbs towards the little white-washed church, a building to which Alfred Watkins gave great significance when working out his ley lines.[16] Past the church there is a cattle grid, and the lane continues through it, running above the west bank of the Edw and heading due south.

There is another way to reach this point from Aberedw Hill. Instead of going north-east from Tabor Wye, take the track that descends the hill by its eastern slopes. This brings you to

106509   Pen-blaen Farm. From here take the footpath that runs east along the northern edge of a small wood. This will bring you to another farm track; turn right along it and you come out on the

120505   lane from Cregrina. A footpath on the other side of the lane brings you to a bridge across the Edw, a little to the north of Gilfach village. Turn right here, passing a primitive methodist chapel and a telephone box until you see a lane sign-posted to Rhulen.

The walks running east from Rhulen are given on pages 188-90. For the purpose of this walk, you must leave the road by the steep track that runs to your right. This brings you to the gate for

133496   Llanbedr Hill. Once through it you are confronted by three tracks. Ignore the one on your extreme left which runs straight up the hill.

The central one runs initially through a small pass on the side of the hill, climbs to one of its highest points, leaves the farm of Ireland on its north-east and descends towards Painscastle.

154476   When the way divides take the central track. This soon becomes a roadway, which enters the village from the north by the Maesllwch Arms.

The right-hand path from the gate runs round the side of the hill. If you follow it, you have another choice to make when you

125482   reach a junction of paths. From here you can either descend the hill to the south-east or make a longer walk by continuing

116477   westwards between the supine Cradle Rocks. Here again you

Aberedw Hill

185

can choose the left-hand path down the southern slopes of Llandeilo Hill or continue a little further to the west.

If you take the second course you may be able to find a trace of the grave of the legendary Twm Tobacco. Just under a mile from Cradle Rocks you come to a place where two tracks cross. On your right you will see a boundary stone. This indicates that this place was once an important cross-roads, just the sort of place where a felon was traditionally buried. The mystery is that although Twm Tobacco's name is known with affection by everyone in these parts, no one seems to know anything about him. Francis Kilvert, the Victorian diarist curate of near-by Clyro (see page 221), asked who he was with as little success as I have had. John Hunt of Llandrindod Wells has given me the most satisfactory explanation. He believes that this Tom may not have been a brigand, despite his burial place, but a packman, who would have been very popular and well-respected if he carried tobacco in those unenlightened days. In that case 'the grave' may mark the place where he was murdered for his wares and money, or where he may have met his death from exhaustion. If this is the case, then the drovers must have known him too, and may well have played a part in ensuring that his memory still lives.

Here you must take the track on your left, which like the other descends to the south and will bring you out on a lane to the west of Painscastle. The advantage of this particular track is that it comes out opposite the farm of Pen-y-graig, where, if you are lucky, you will see the majestic, four-horned, piebald Jacob sheep. Sleek and magnificent they look beside their speckled-faced Welsh companions. Some people believe that these sheep were brought to Britain from the wrecks of the Spanish Armada, so it is possible that they would be known to the drovers. You are now about six miles (9.6 kilometres) from Painscastle.

The shorter walk from Cradle Rocks is an interesting and pleasant alternative. I am indebted to John Hunt of Llandrindod Wells, who suggested that it should be included. At the junction of the paths take the one that runs almost due south along a valley. Behind you there is a small lake backed by rocks. Continue down the valley beneath the spectacular rocks, which

Francis Kilvert of Clyro referred to as the Rocks of Pen Cwm. He saw them for the first time on July 3rd, 1872, when he went to visit the Reverend John Price, Master of Arts of Cambridge University and vicar of Llanbedr Painscastle. This eccentric character was generally known as the Solitary. He lived in squalor, confusion and dirt which Kilvert found 'almost inconceivable'. In complete indifference to his surroundings the Solitary showed 'the natural simplicity of the highest breeding'. This man was Kilvert's guide to the famous Rocks of Pen Cwm, and he was properly appreciative. This is how he recorded the event in his diary:

Suddenly we came in sight of the precipitous grey rocks, which are so like the Rocks of Aberedw and which were the last haunt of the fairies, the last place where the little people were seen. Then there was the gleam of silver over the dark heather stems and Llanbychllyn Pool lay in its hollow like a silver shield. The view was beautiful and we all lay down upon the dry heather just budding into pink blossom to enjoy the fair prospect in full view of the grey rocks and the silver lake. And the curlews called and the plovers whistled with their strange wild whistle about the sunny hill.

132471 From those magic rocks the path goes down to the farm lane of Penbedw, and from there to the village of Llanbedr, two miles (3.2 kilometres) west of Painscastle.

The herds from Tabor Wye that were going north-east to Glascwm and Kington would also have had to go over Aberedw Hill to Hungry Green. From here some of them might have gone on to the shoeing station of Cregrina but others would have gone more directly north to the great droving centre of Colva, where they would have been joined by beasts from the north.

121535 To reach the northerly route, turn right along Hungry Green until you come to the footpath over the hill on your left. This path goes through several fields and bears all the marks of once having been a green lane. It has banks surmounted by sparse hawthorn trees on either side of it. It is now very rarely used and is almost completely overgrown in many places. Just before
126545 it reaches the top of the hill, it comes out on a track above the farm of Pen-rhiw. Turn right here and you are on the route for

Glascwm which is given on page 179.

138499

For the southern route to Kington, follow the lane from
Cregrina until you reach the signpost for Rhulen. The village
lies in a steep valley and consists of two or three cottages by a
bridge and a tiny church, dedicated to St David, with an odd
coffin-shaped door. This church stands on what would seem to
be a prehistoric man-made eminence. At the north of the village
an ancient, tree-canopied hollow way climbs to the east. Take it

Flooded grass

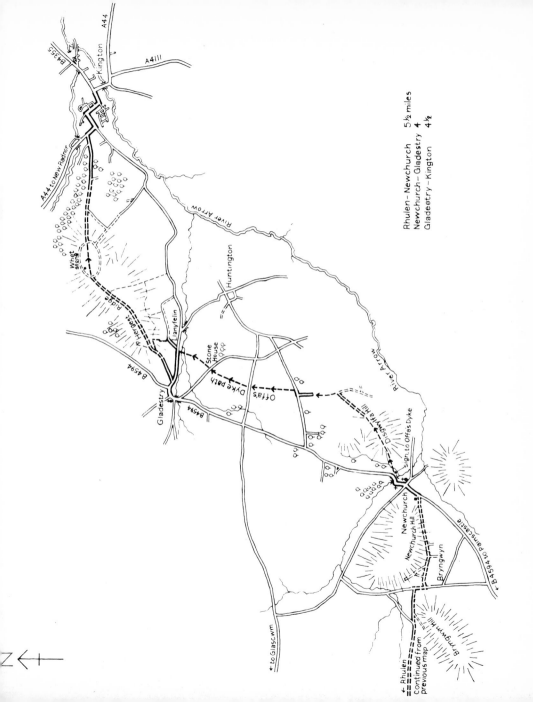

Map O

Rhulen – Newchurch   5½ miles
Newchurch – Gladestry   4
Gladestry – Kington   4½

N

Kington
A44
A4111
B4355
A44 to New Radnor
River Arrow
Wheat stand
Hergest Ridge
B4594
Llanfelin
Huntington
Stone House
Offa's Dyke Path
Gladestry
B4594
River Arrow
Disgwylfa Hill
Sign. to Offa's Dyke
Newchurch
Newchurch Hill
Bryngwyn
B4594 to Painscastle
Bryngwyn Hill
To Glascwm
Rhulen
Continued from previous map

Map O page 189
145504

187504

to join a farm lane leading to Pentre Farm; when you have passed that building, you will be on a track that runs due east across the hills for some three miles (4.8 kilometres).

On its last stages this track runs round the northern slopes of Bryngwyn Hill. When it reaches a lane running north/south, go south a little way and then pick up the track running east. This is now a very clearly marked cattle road. It goes south of Newchurch Hill, and comes out at a farm a little below the village.

When you cross the bridge to the north of Newchurch, you will see a sign to Offa's Dyke on your right. Take the Dyke path to Stone House, where a bridleway across the road brings you to Llanyfelin just to the east of Gladestry. Here you can either continue along the path to the north or turn left into the village. If you do visit the village, leave it by the bridge by the inn and then take the minor road running due east. You very soon leave this for a track on your left, which climbs steeply up to Hergest Ridge to join the Dyke path.

This ridgeway runs directly to the east past the strange, irregular triangle of the Whet Stone, with the marks of an ancient race track around it. The origins of the Whet Stone are almost as mysterious as those of Twm Tobacco. There is even a legend that at cock crow this stone rolls down to the brook to drink, and then climbs back to its old position. Some people believe that it was used as an exchange stone at the time of the Black Death, and marks the place where people from plague-struck villages might come to leave their goods. This tradition is mentioned in an 1845 *History of Kington*, by Richard Parry, and is quoted by Alfred Watkins, who obviously reckoned that the stone's main importance was as a way mark.[17] He believed that it and other similarly named stones were so called because they defined an 'old sighted track of the ancient whetstone pedlar'. Whether that is so or not, the stone must have been an important landmark to the drovers.

The track over the hill ends at a gate leading into a lane running beside a wood. This lane will bring you out on to the main road a little to the west of Kington.

Church door, Rhulen

Llandovery

(Ordnance Survey sheets 146/147/148/160)

Toll House, Pumpsaint

Tregaron is still an important market centre, but it was in the first half of the nineteenth century that it really flourished. Then the shoeing station was able to keep at least half a dozen smiths busy, and the big dealers in the area sometimes employed nearly a score of drovers. In fact, as one of those drovers said to George Borrow, the town was 'not quite so big as London, but a very good place'.

When Borrow visited the town, he stayed at the Talbot Arms. Dr Richard Colyer has recorded that the cattle were collected in a field behind that inn.[18] It was from here that many of the cattle and sheep that were herded along the drove routes described in the following pages started their journey east. Some of the Tregaron drovers only went as far as Hereford, but they were concerned solely with sheep. Throughout the nineteenth century the flocks were gathered into the town from the outlying villages as soon as Sunday midnight had struck. Then, late on Monday night or in the early hours of Tuesday morning, the drovers set out with their flocks, going via Abergwesyn, Beulah and Brecon. They only allowed themselves three hours rest at night and, returning by the way they had gone, they were back in Tregaron by the following Friday.

Although you should visit Tregaron, you will probably find that the best way to follow the trails of the Cardiganshire runts is to base yourself first in the Lampeter/Llandovery area and then to move into Hereford from Builth Wells.

The Tregaron herds were joined by the cattle from the rich lands of the west coast (where the mid-Wales sheep and cattle

Opposite Five Saints stone,
Pumpsaint
Above and left Dolaucothi gold
mine

were often sent for fattening). From the wide fertile valley of the lower reaches of the Tywi, as it flows through Carmarthen and Llandeilo, cattle and sheep converged on Pumpsaint (five saints). It lies on the road from Lampeter (through which the Tregaron herds came) and from Llandeilo to the south. The eighteenth- and nineteenth-century drovers had to pay a toll on the road here, but after that payment most of them contrived to avoid any further tolls until they crossed into England. At Pumpsaint the cattle were shod for their long journey over the mountains. The old forge in the village is a garage now.

The drove route east from Pumpsaint runs through the Roman gold mines of the Cothi valley. These were worked on and off until 1939. Follow the A482 east for a few hundred yards, and then take the first lane on your left after you have crossed the Cothi river. This brings you into the Dolaucothi valley, most of which is now owned by the National Trust. It is here that you will find the stone of the five saints to whom Pumpsaint owes its name. From these gold mines many of the drovers took bullion to the London dealers.

From Dolaucothi two choices present themselves. You can either immediately start to follow the path of the main cattle droves to the east or you can take a look at the wild country to the north and west, from which the cattle, sheep and even geese were driven to Pumpsaint and Cilycwm.

If you take the second alternative, Defoe gives you some idea of the sort of land you will be traversing:

The principal river is the Towy, which runs among the impassable mountains, which range along the centre of this part of Wales, and which we call impassable, for that even the people themselves call'd them so; we looked at them indeed with astonishment, for their rugged tops and the immense height of them ... Some think it's from the impassable mountains of this country that we have an old saying that the devil lives in the midst of Wales.[19]

The territory that you'll be exploring here once lay under the dominion of the Tregaron-born Twm Sion Catti, a drover who flourished in the late sixteenth century. He married a Brecon

Twm Sion Catti's cave

heiress and became mayor of that city. He had the grace to remember her in his will, dated May 17th, 1609, which was quoted by R. I. Davies in the publication of the Cardiganshire Antiquary Society for 1927. He left 'to my base son John Moy the nine head of cattle, and the residue to my wife Johan Jones'. He was a real enough man, but the legends of his Robin Hood exploits were mainly invented in the 1820s by a writer called Llewelyn Pritchard. You can see the cave where he was reputed to have had his hide-out. It stands on a cliff face in part of the R.S.P.B. reserve, at 786466, just off the new road to the reservoir of Llyn Brianne.

Map P page 196

From Cellan (612496) on the east bank of the Teifi as it runs north from Lampeter to Cilycwm (752400)

This is a good day's walk, and well to the south of the youth hostels. If you are not camping, your best bet would be to stay at one of the many bed-and-breakfast houses in Lampeter. I believe that some drovers from Tregaron would have taken their animals across the easily fordable Teifi, just above Cellan, in order to save paying the tolls at Lampeter Bridge, and to keep the beasts away from the traffic and the other herds in the very busy market town. If you walk along the road a little way to the north from Cellan village, until the river runs by the road, you will soon see a gate on your right. The gate leads into a field, but the old track runs along the side of it, until it meets a farm access road. Follow this round the hill, until after skirting a bit of forestry land it comes out on the Sarn Helen – the ancient road adapted by the Romans. This stretch of it can be used by cars. Follow it south-east for about two miles (3.2 kilometres), then when the road (now no longer straight and Roman) drops due south, take a track through the hills to the east. Before you do so, it's worthwhile looking at two cairns. One is either a cap-stone or a fallen monolith lying in a small circular earthwork. It lies to the west of the road, just after the track branches off to the east. The other is on top of a hill, just to the north of the track. This is the circular 'beehive' type of cairn, made up of small stones. The easterly track goes straight over the hill, and descends the sharp incline on the other side at an angle of forty-five degrees. This path was put into its present shape 150 years ago, when the farmer who used that land ploughed the way down the hill so that the track would be wide

616498

635503

646481

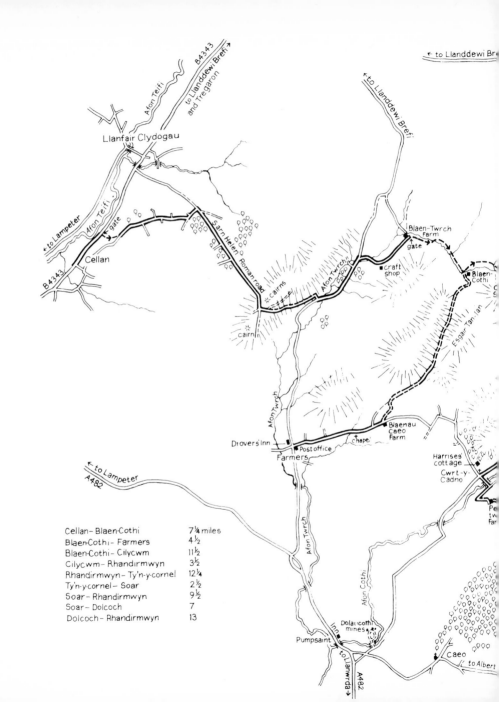

N

to Llanddewi Bre

B4343

Aton Teifi

to Llanddewi Brefi
and Tregaron

to Llanddewi Brefi

Llanfair Clydogau

to Lampeter

Aton Teifi

gate

Cellan

B4343

Sarn Helen Roman road

cairns

cairn

Blaen-Twrch
Farm

gate

Craft
shop

Aton Twrch

Blaen-
Cothi

Esgair Tan-lan

Aton Twrch

Drovers Inn

Post office

Farmers

chapel

Blaenau
Caeo
Farm

Harrises
cottage

Cwrt-y-
Cadno

to Lampeter
A482

Aton Twrch

Aton Cothi

Pe
tw
Far

Dolaucothi
mines

Pumpsaint

Inn

to Llanwrda

A482

Caeo

to Albert

Cellan – Blaen-Cothi   7¼ miles
Blaen-Cothi – Farmers   4½
Blaen-Cothi – Cilycwm   11½
Cilycwm – Rhandirmwyn   3½
Rhandirmwyn – Ty'n-y-cornel   12¼
Ty'n-y-cornel – Soar   2½
Soar – Rhandirmwyn   9½
Soar – Dolcoch   7
Dolcoch – Rhandirmwyn   13

Map P

enough to take the carts carrying grain to the mill at the bottom. The mill house still stands there, but it is many years since any flour was ground in this valley.

Turn left along the road in the valley, and follow it across the mill stream and through a wood. Just after you come out of the wood take the lane on your right. The house at the top of the hill is a rather unusual craft centre run by Jerry and Judith Hoad, who specialize entirely in work made by local craftsmen.

673489

The wood-carving, knitting and weaving that you will find here are quite different to the sort of things you will see displayed in the tourist craft shops in all Welsh towns.

682496 Carry on down the lane from the Hoads' house to the farm of Blaen-Twrch. It stands at the point where the Twrch valley narrows and where it is joined by one of the many rivulets that form the source of the Cothi. The way you'll be following now is the way that pigs were taken on the first part of their journey to Cilycwm.

Left and below left Beehive cairn You will see a gate at the end of the lane, just after you have walked past the farm. The gate is blocked up now so you must climb over it; then take the path on your right as it runs along the south side of the stream.

The pig path running east soon crosses to the north of the stream and follows the contours of the hills, winding in an easterly direction. You will find that it frequently disappears and, as this land is very marshy, the most sensible thing is simply to follow the dry land round the curves of the hills, keeping the Cothi stream on your right. You will have to cross one other stream running north, and then as you round the hill 695487 of Bryn Ceiliogau you will see the ruin of Blaen-Cothi cottage.

The cottage and its grounds are sometimes used for shearing now, but half a century ago it was inhabited by one Dai O'Ajax (a descendant, they say, of the Phoenicians who came to find gold in Cornwall, and eventually followed the news of more prosperous gold mines across the Bristol Channel into Wales). His main business at Blaen-Cothi was the rearing of geese, and after the valley farmers had harvested their oats he would take them down the mountain to Pumpsaint, so that they could fatten on the gleanings and the rich lowland pastures before being taken to the autumn markets. The path they would have taken is reached by crossing the Cothi and heading south along the westerly slopes of Esgair Tan-lan, by some new forestry plantations, and then descending the mountainside fairly steeply to the farm of Blaenau Caeo.

650447 The road to the right here goes past the chapel to the village of Farmers, which is so called because what is now the post-office shop was at one time the Farmers' Inn. Across the road the Drovers' Inn still stands. The haggling and business arrangements took place in the road between them, and a busy cross-roads it must have been, with the blacksmith's field at the north-east corner of it. The story goes that the geese who came to these meadows after the hard living of Blaen-Cothi were for ever falling on their backs, for they tugged too hard at the lush lowland grass which surprised them by coming away very easily.

The pigs were also on their way to a good feed. Still keeping north of the stream, they passed the rocky outcrop of Crug Siarls (Charles' Rock), so called because in Cromwellian times cattle from the lowland farm of Esgerwen in the valley by Llansewel were hidden here, so that they shouldn't be rounded up for the soldiers. Past Crug Siarls you will come to an occupied farm of Nantyrast, and from there a steep but made-up lane runs north of the Cothi around the edge of Banc y Garth to the deserted farm of Garthynty. It was here that the pigs were pastured, and the Garthynty farmer made the grazing of these herds a major part of his business. From Garthynty the lane crosses a stream and climbs to run just above the Cothi, which is particularly beautiful at this point. The road goes through a gate and then across a cattle grid to descend steeply by the farm of Bwlch-y-rhiw, where it enters the macadamized road.

730465

You will often find that the drove tracks were also used by pilgrims of one sort or another, and the pig path is no exception. People came along it from Lampeter to visit the chapel which lies across the road a little to the east of Bwlch-y-rhiw. It is beautifully set in a small wood by a stream and, although it has been restored twice, it probably didn't look very different when it was first put up in 1797. Why people should have made such a journey to reach it I have yet to discover. Was there some very notable preacher there? Or was it some way of avoiding the legislation which confined worshippers to their own region? The pigs are a clearer matter. They went to the south-west, following the banks of the Cothi until they came to the village of Cwrt-y-Cadno. For generations a family of Harrises, with extraordinary powers of wisdom and cunning, lived in the cottage opposite the chapel. The most powerful wizard of them all lived in the sixteenth century and it was he, folk tell you,

693443

Opposite and left Crug Siarls
Below Pig grazing grounds at
Garthynty

who split the megalith on the hill to the east of that village. You
will see the stone, for it stands on the track to Cilycwm.

To reach it take the lane marked 'No Through Road' just by the
telephone box. This little lane crosses a stream and comes to a T
junction. Here you take the right-hand lane to Mr Williams's
695437 farm of Pen-twyn. A track way goes through the farmyard
along the north side of a wooded valley owned by the National
Trust. This goes through several gates, the last of which brings
you out to the mountainside of Esgair Ferchon. It is here that
you will find the wizard-smitten stone.

Take the track to the right that runs along the south side of the
mountain. (There is a much more clearly marked track running
more sharply to the right, but you must ignore that. It is of
recent origin, and leads directly to the forest.) The path you
want keeps the forest on your right and the steep sides of the
hill to your left. When it starts to climb over the ridge of the hill
towards the valley to the north, take the right-hand path.
This runs along the south side of a small wood, and eventually
brings you out to a couple of fields. Cross these as you go down
hill towards the stream and farm house, and from there to the
lane a few yards to the north of the village of Cilycwm.

This route was used as a drove route within living memory, but it was sheep – not pigs – that were taken along it. Mr. Williams's father took sheep from Pen-twyn along this way, on the first part of his three-day journey to Gower. On the first day he would get as far as Llandeilo. He told his son that the secret of successful droving was to make very early starts each morning.

A round trip from Rhandirmwyn (785438)

There is much to see in this area, and as the three youth hostels are conveniently placed, you could spend two or three days on this trip.

797440
776446

Split megalith south of Cwrt-y-Cadno

From the Rhandirmwyn hostel, make your way along the path which runs north-west to the village of Nantybai. From there turn right to cross the Tywi by an ugly and rather tourist-ridden bridge – the pub by the bridge keeps peacocks. From now on you are on the path along which, had you been walking it some 150 years ago, you might well have met the black cattle or flocks of sheep coming south-eastwards from Llanddewi Brefi to Cilycwm.

764450

You will be keeping mainly on a north-westerly course. Follow the road for a little while to your right until you come to a lane leading to the right by a very sharp bend. After this lane crosses a bridge you follow it to the left into a reserve owned by the R.S.P.B. This means that you must keep to the paths and walk reasonably quietly. The droves would have come down the track that is now a metalled road climbing up the east side of the first valley you come to, but for a prettier walk cross the valley and enter its westerly side, by a path that branches off from an inhabited farm house. The path immediately enters a little wood, and then starts to climb up the side of the valley towards the point where the metalled road becomes a stone track.

755474

Follow this track to the standing stone, a large flat one, at the edge of the forest, where you will see on the mountainside one surprisingly green field.

The track now follows the edge of the forest, along its south-west side, but because a great deal of new planting is going on in this area you will soon run into new forestry roads. When you pass the grown forest, cross the new road and carry on north-west near the top of Cefn Gwenffrwd. The road slowly winds down into the valley, which is dominated to the south-east by the sinister rocks of Craig Pysgotwr. You will have some difficulty in making your way down to the stream that runs through this valley now, for the whole of this mountainside has been planted with a new crop of conifers. But, having come into the valley, it is quite easy to see where the old track fords the stream, and on its northern bank the old road shows quite clearly running along the side of Hafod Lâs. The path brings

7549

737504

you into the pass between that hill and a slightly smaller one to the north-west. Here you can see several grass mounds, which look rather like oddly placed earthworks, but are locally reported to be the ruins of an old drovers' inn. From here the

736514 path is clear, though muddy, to the farm of Bryn-glas – a happily inhabited holding, where the farmer is building a new barn and shearing shed, in the old style, with circular stone pillars.

The farm road goes across the river, and you turn left along the macadam road into which it leads. Follow this for just over a mile (1.6 kilometres) until the sign on your right directs you to

751535 the Youth Hostel at Ty'n-y-cornel. You are now on the route along which most of the cattle from Llanddewi Brefi would have been driven, and as you turn to the south-east, you are going along the same track that the droves would have taken.

785534 From the Youth Hostel the road runs due east to Soar chapel, reputed to be the most isolated chapel in Wales, and one to which farmers from all over this wide moorland would have made their way on horseback. For many people in these isolated farms, chapel-going must have been the only occasion when they spoke to people outside their own households. Now Soar is simply used once a year for an annual summer service, but it is always open to visitors. From Soar there are two choices. You can either return immediately to Rhandirmwyn, or you can go a longer way round staying, if time serves, at the newly opened

810565 hostel at Dolgoch, by the source of the Tywi. The hostel is a reconstructed farm house and is open all the year round, despite its isolated situation.

To take the shorter route, which is the one taken by the Llanddewi Brefi herds, follow the track to the south-east, taking the right-hand path when it divides. This brings you to the

783524 inhabited farm of Nant-llwyd, which was once the centre of quite a large community. The ruins of twenty-eight squatters' farms (shelters put up on common ground and built within twenty-four hours gave the inhabitant right of tenure) have been counted in this region. From Nant-llwyd the path runs south-west through the pass between Foel Fraith and the high point of Pen y Gurnos to the banks of the Doethie. From this point it follows the stream fairly closely due south until the

765483   Doethie joins the Pysgotwr. You now follow the northerly bank of the river as it runs south-east; after a mile (1.6 kilometres) or so you will find that you can cross the stream to its south side, 775472   and so on to a path that runs first south and then south-west until you cross the river and join a lane to the north of Rhandirmwyn.

763576   The other road from Soar first runs north-west along a rather dull macadam road, through Maes-glas to join the mountain road between Tregaron and Abergwesyn, the most widely used drove route in the west of Wales. Where the Soar road meets it by the river, you will find the ruined walls of small pens. The sheep on their way east were driven into these, and from them were forced to swim the Camddwr River. Without these pens, they would simply have spread over the mountainside when they came to the water.

804572   You must now follow the mountain road up hill about four miles (6.4 kilometres) to the east, to the river that flows due south into the new reservoir of Llyn Brianne. If you follow this stream along its westerly bank for about a mile (1.6 kilometres) 810565   the track will bring you to the Youth Hostel.

805537   You are now on the route which the herds from Aberystwyth and Ffair Rhos would have taken to join the herds of Cilycwm. Some would have gone south into Glamorgan, and so crossed into England from the Aust passage to Bristol. From the Youth Hostel, you can follow the track down for about two miles (3.2 kilometres) until it meets the forestry road. Cross the bridge to the east side of the river, and follow the forestry road back to Rhandirmwyn. Although you are now in the same area as the old drove route, the way has been completely lost with the flooding of the valley and the planting of the conifers. Don't take this road at weekends or at the height of the holiday season, when it becomes packed with tourists who come to see the dam at the southern end of the reservoir.

786467   About a mile and a half (2.4 kilometres) from the dam on the right-hand side of the road, opposite the farm of Ystradffin, you will find the R.S.P.B. nature reserve, with a clearly marked trail leading you to the famous cave of Twm Sion Catti. Then it is about three and a half miles (5.6 kilometres) to Rhandirmwyn.

On the road from Tregaron to
Abergwesyn

From Pumpsaint and the Dolaucothi mines, the route to
Cilycwm that the droves from the south would have followed
runs by the lanes to Caeo and Albert Mount. After Tregaron,
Caeo was the most important western centre for cattle dealing,
and many notable drovers came from there. We have records of
one from the eighteenth century. Dafydd Jones was a well-
known figure at Barnet and Maidstone fairs, and he made use
of his time in the east to learn English. The story goes that
he became an ardent Christian, after his conversion in the
hills about six miles (9.6 kilometres) from Llanfair-ym-
muallt. From that moment, he started to use the English he
picked up in his trade for the task of translating the hymns of
Isaac Watts for his fellow-Welshmen. He seems to have led a
prosperous life, and when he gave up droving he settled in a
small farm near Esgerdawe, known as Llundain Fach (Little
London) and bordered by a stream which he referred to as the
Thames.

685399 From Caeo, take the lane which runs steeply up hill between
the inn and the post-office shop, and after a mile and a half (2.4
690394 kilometres) you will come to a farm on your right called Albert
Mount. There is another house beside it, and opposite that a
gate into the field. This leads into a track which runs along the
top of a hill to bring you into a short hollow way, a narrow
overgrown path between high hedges, which possibly marked a
boundary. The cattle would have been driven this way, and in
more recent times, before children were taken to school by bus
and taxi, the pupils of Caeo school came along here on their way
to and from the outlying farms to the north-east. Mrs James,
who now helps her husband farm at Benlan near Porthyrhyd in

Hollow way, near Caeo

the next valley, spent her childhood at Nant-iwrch, and vividly
remembers the walk to school and the delights of the changing
seasons. But it may be a case of the past always being golden,
for in the snow and mists it must have been quite a hard walk.

The grass hollow way comes out into a little narrow lane
opposite an empty cottage just to the west of a cross-roads.
698395   Cross the stream and go north-west; when the lane forks, do not
follow the sign to Mrs James's old home of Nant-iwrch on your
right, but go along the road on your left which follows a stream
towards the farm of Llwyn-Owen. Go on past that farm, along
the side of the hill, until you come to the last farm in this valley
714403   Blaendyffryn. Do not go as far as the farm, but keep to the right
lane which soon becomes a rough track. When you come to a
stream on your left, leave the track and turn across the stream

723394

744402

to enter the southern part of Caeo Forest. Keep to the main forest road which runs south-east to bring you out on the slopes of Pen Lifau. Turn right and walk along the edge of the forest until you come to a farm lane. Follow this past two farms and, keeping to the road as it runs to your left, follow it round as it swerves right for the village of Cilycwm. The footpath marked on the O.S. map from the farm of Cwm-Fran-fawr to the chapel in the village is unfortunately lost.

Cilycwm was a collecting place for the cattle from these hills. In the village street you can still see the man-made water course running in front of the houses, which was designed to provide water for the animals before they continued their journey and was sometimes used as a general feeding trough. A little while ago the Council wanted to widen this road and fill in the old water course; but the villagers were proud of their history, and happily refused to let that happen. Follow the road out towards the east. It runs to the north of the church, which is worth a visit for its wall paintings – the one on the west wall, a Skeleton, dates from the fifteenth century.

There is nothing for it now but to stay with this minor road, past the now disused brick kilns of Cynghordy, which were closed in 1975, across the Bran, and so to the main Llandovery road. Turn to the right and go a little way along the main road towards the town. On your right here is the Cynghordy Inn, known to the drovers as the Talgarth Inn, and oddly so, for Talgarth itself lies well to the east. Yet the local people still refer to the publican as Taylor of Talgarth, for that is the name of the farm which makes up the main part of this pub. This arrangement was common at the time when inns and farms were often run by the one family. Although the drovers who patronized the Talgarth Inn would have gone straight east from here towards the village of Tirabad, and we shall eventually follow their tracks, this is probably the time to take a look at Llandovery itself, and the part that the town played in cattle dealing, by which it was largely shaped.

It was the seventeenth-century vicar of Llandovery, Rees Pritchard, born in 1575 and author of *The Welshman's Candle*, who let us know how drovers were regarded in his day. In his poem he exhorts a drover 'to be honest in his dealings, to fulfil

Left Near Cilycwm
Below Cilycwm

his promise, to refrain from imbibing too freely, and to drop the habit of absconding with his employer's money to Ireland and the low countries'. (I owe this translation to G. D. Owen, who quoted from Vicar Pritchard's words in his contribution to the 1939 *History of Carmarthenshire*.[20]) Not that the vicar himself had all his life been clear of the vices he warned the drovers against. He was a memorable drunk, before his rather unusual conversion on being confronted by an alcoholic goat. George Borrow records that before that happened, his parishioners would say, 'Bad as we may be, we are not half as bad as the parson.'[21]

King's Head Inn

The real effect that the drovers had on Llandovery, however, belongs to the history of banking. The Bank of the Black Ox was founded in 1799 by David Jones, a farmer's son, who is sometimes described as a drover. The bank was started in the King's Head Inn, which in its turn is now making a small fortune out of the drovers with its Twm Sion Catti bars and its piped music. According to Roy Saunders, who wrote about the Llandovery Black Ox Bank in *The Western Mail* of February 25th, 1935, David Jones was employed at the age of fifteen at the King's Head, where the cattle dealers fell into the habit of asking him to look after their money. His career took a more ambitious turn when he married a lady with a fortune of £10,000. By the time of his death in 1839, he had multiplied that by five, and had become High Sheriff of Carmarthen, a post to which he was appointed in 1820. After his death, the business was carried on by his three grandsons, David, William and John. David had the bank at Llandovery, William at Lampeter and John at Llandeilo. In Llandovery the bank is now run by Lloyds from the same building, Prospect House in the High Street, to which the family moved it in 1903. The Joneses' bank continued to issue cheques marked with the black ox until early in the First World War.

Prospect House

Your best link now with the drovers in the town lies in the recently built auction shed at one corner of the cattle market beneath the castle ruins. The building may be new, but when you hear stock auctioned here it is not difficult to imagine how these transactions would have taken place two or three hundred years ago. In the Castle Inn by the cattle market, you can always find a list of dates for the forthcoming stock sales. They are worth attending.

The cattle which collected at Llandovery would have been driven east, along what is now the A40, towards Brecon. It is best not to follow the droves along this way, particularly during the holiday season when the road can be just a queue of cars. Nor did they go all the way into Brecon, where the tolls were particularly heavy. Instead they turned left at Pentrebach and Trecastle to journey north and join the herds from Cilycwm at Tirabad, for the crossing of the great upland mass of the Eppynt. Once again, one cannot really follow them on that northerly part. For one thing, the Forestry Commission now owns most of that land and so the original drove routes are obscured. But more seriously, the army training camp at Sennybridge, which operates over the whole of the Eppynt plateau, has put large areas of the zone out of reach of the public for great stretches of time. Although you can walk across the ranges when the red flags are not flying, and although the army will let you know in advance what weekends are free from training practice, it is possibly best to give this whole area a fairly wide berth. In any case, many of the ancient trackways are concreted over now, and there are still the odd explosives lying about.

Some two hundred years ago, when John Clark drew up his memorandum on the state of agriculture in the county of Brecknock, he also had sad things to say about the Eppynt. He described it as 'a wide range of barren and uncultivated mountains (which) would, for the most part of the way, chill the philanthropic breast with dejection and excite compassion for that portion of its kindred race whose inauspicious fate had destined them to become tenants of this inhospitable region'. The philanthropic breast cannot take any greater cheer today. However, this need not stop you reflecting on the richness of the agricultural landscape of Breconshire as a whole. Daniel Defoe, who suffered no restrictions of traffic or military exercises, found Breconshire a wild and terrible county, more fit to be called 'Breakneckshire'. Yet, 'Tho this county be so mountainous,' he wrote, 'provisions are exceedingly plentiful, and also very good all over the country; nor are those mountains useless, even to the city of London, as I have noted of other counties, for from hence they send yearly great herds of black cattle to

England, and which are known to fill our fairs and markets even that of Smithfield itself.'[2 2]

Breconshire has always been in the forefront of agricultural advance. The county's agricultural society was founded in the eighteenth century at a meeting in the Golden Lion Inn in the county town; and the farming practice of that time is popularly believed to have been much advanced by the energies of Howell Harris, who managed to combine enthusiastic Christian evangelism with most effective farming techniques. There is a museum devoted to his work at his old home at Trefecca, between Brecon and Builth Wells, and here you can see evidence of the two obsessions that ruled his life.

Long before the eighteenth century, it is reported that some unnamed Breconshire ploughman added a mould board to his plough, and because of this his descendants were able to become masters of the straight furrow. There must be some truth in the story, for it is backed by hard cash. At one time a premium of ten guineas a year was being offered to farm servants from other counties in Wales who were prepared to go and live in Breconshire for three years to learn the art of ploughing. John Clark reported that 'every ploughman here is perfectly master of the straight line, for every ridge runs mathematically true.'

Today Breconshire (now Powys) has one farming practice that concerns the walker. The region is exempted from the law which prohibits farmers in other areas from allowing bulls to run over rights of way. This is partly because you will find few fields here; most of the country is open moorland. The bulls you will come across are mainly Herefords, which although they look like bison are reported to be gentle enough when they are running with the cows. In any case, you would have more to fear from a cow with a recently born calf, who can be quite ferocious if she imagines that her offspring is threatened. Bulls, by the way, cannot see colours, so don't worry about red rags. It is much more important to remember to keep fairly quiet and not to run. It is sudden unexpected noises or movements that can set off trouble.

With these matters in mind, let's go back to the Talgarth Inn on the road to Llanwrtyd-Wells and find the track of the

Cilycwm herds as they would have gone by Tirabad church. Unless you want a long walk through the forestry roads and along Cefn Llwydlo, the path of the grey calf, it is best to follow the road to Tirabad, an ugly modern village made up of Forestry Commission houses and army married quarters. Its name does not celebrate some eastern military victory, as one might think, but is in fact Welsh for 'the lands of the abbot', another indication that monks as well as cattle would sometimes have come this way from Strata Florida.

8542
878414

At one time the village consisted simply of the farm of Llandulas, which stands across a narrow lane going up into the Eppynt Mountains, and runs alongside the old church. There were two near-by pubs: the Cross Inn, well known to the drovers as they made their way up to the Eppynt, and Spite Inn, which was opened lower down in the valley, to spite the Cross Inn, or so they say. Cross Inn lies under forest now, but the lady who has lived at Llandulas Farm for the last forty years, and who has seen the new village grow up around her, was born there, and affirms that the lane is little changed from the one the drovers would have known … apart from the fir trees which now surround it.

It was at her farm that a certain Rhys Williams once worked in the shoeing meadow. According to an article on cattle tracks written on January 17th, 1935, and to be found in Brecon Museum, he 'was able to find sufficient work for himself and three others in making cattle cues and false coins, which he sold to the drovers, who managed to pass them as good money at the centres they visited'. Another person well remembered here was a wealthy cattle dealer called John Davies, who employed about a dozen drovers to take his herds to the east and who ran a shoeing station on his farm.

9347

If you don't want to risk the Eppynt ranges, there is nothing for it but to take the road due north from the village and make your way to Llangammarch Wells. As you go you might like to reflect on how the march of the black cattle struck the imagination of Brecon's local historian, John Lloyd:

A fine sight that must have been along the sloping roadway up the mountain side, the deep black gorge at Cwmydwfnant

The Drovers' Arms, Eppynt
Heights

beneath, and the purple heather-clad banks on either side. I have ridden along this sloping mountainside roadway – but have never seen the droves of big majestic black oxen passing up in single file in an almost endless procession. It must have been a grand sight, the massive jet black beasts leisurely labouring upwards with here and there in view a single horseman in charge, and then would come the thought that none of these thousands of cattle would ever return.[2 3]

The Welsh blacks would never have been massive, as John Lloyd must have known, for he distinctly remembers 'meeting the drovers near Llanspythid – and thought – I was quite young then – or perhaps I should now, what a wondrous sight to see the black crowd marching forward'.[2 4] But no matter, he did a good job of translating the wonders of his childhood for us, and in 1903 he could follow it all up by welcoming the fact that 'on the Eppynt range the old track is quite open and ready for use at the present time.'[2 5] To which we can only say, 'Would that it were so.'

The Eppynt range is best avoided now. Although there are some weekends when the army is not using it, and you can find out when these are from the Brecon Beacons National Park information centre in Brecon or from the military camp at Sennybridge, there are always explosives lying around, and it's not wise to venture off the army roads. Most of the time a red flag system operates, and whenever the flags are flying it means that the ranges are in active use. But this system is more for motorists than for walkers. On foot you could go on to the ranges when the flags were down, but when they went up you

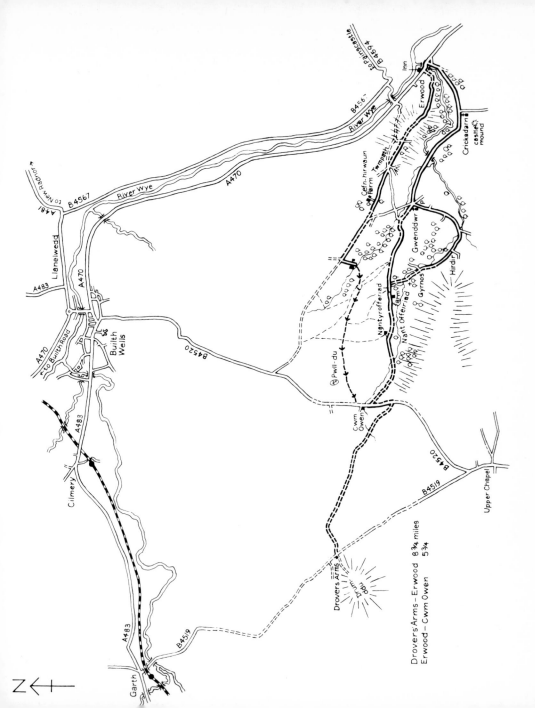

Map Q

might well not have time to get clear.

Map Q page 215
986452

If you are doing this part of the trip by car, you could take up the story again at the Drovers' Arms. This lies on the Eppynt Heights about five miles (eight kilometres) south of Garth on the road to Upper Chapel. It is now a sad-looking building on the right-hand side of the road. It has just acquired a new corrugated-iron roof, the previous one having been blown off in the gales of January 1976.

The building is now used as a bivouac for soldiers on manoeuvres, but in its prime it must have been one of the most welcome inns to drovers who had brought cattle up the long slope of the Eppynt. The grandson of the last couple to run it as a hostelry wrote a small pamphlet on the cattle trade, which he called *The Trail of the Black Ox*. It is now unobtainable, but you can see a copy in the library of Brecon Museum. This anonymous historian remembered the halfpenny grazing field where the drovers pastured their cattle overnight; and he recalled how 'the children from the inn on the Eppynt would go to the highest point of their land to see if there were any sign of the cattle approaching. After waiting a little time they would see a man on horseback coming over the horizon, they would wave and shout and the horseman would then blow the horn and wave as the children ran back home to say the cattle were coming.' Here, as at other drovers' inns, the advent of a drove was the sign for general local festivities. Boxing matches were arranged between the farmers and the drovers, and touring fiddlers would add to the general merrymaking.

Cwm Owen Inn

The Eppynt, which is now only inhabited by sheep and soldiers, was a lively place in the nineteenth century. Quite apart from the regular passage of the drovers, the farms in the area were the centre of a busy weaving, knitting and spinning industry. People round here remember those lost farms now, in much the same way as those a little further to the north recall the drowned pastures beneath the Elan and Claerwen reservoirs.

From the Drovers' Arms you can drive directly to the east along the new military concrete until you come to the road between Builth Wells and Upper Chapel (B4520). You are now out of the danger zone. Turn north along this road, and you will see

021443 immediately the small inn of Cwm Owen on your left. The drovers would have known this as an inn, but it is now run as a small tourist café. From here the droves made their way towards the Wye at a ford just to the north of the village of Erwood. If you have come by car, you can leave it at Cwm Owen and make a round walk between here and Erwood.

If you are on foot, you would have given up following the trail at Tirabad and taken the train either from Llanwrtyd Wells or from Llangammarch Wells to Builth Road. From there you can get the Abergavenny bus to Erwood. In that case, start the round walk from that village; it takes about three hours.

To make the walk from Cwm Owen, start off along the track that leaves the main road on your left after you have walked a few hundred yards to the south. This path runs along the side of a stream which it eventually crosses, and then runs due east to Nantyrofferiad Farm and then to Groeswen Farm. From here you can follow the lane through to the villages of Gwenddwr, Crickadarn (with its castle mound and beautiful thirteenth-century church porch) and so to Erwood.

Church porch, Crickadarn

Some of the drovers, however, would have gone a more roundabout way. When you leave the farm of Groeswen, you will find a footpath on your right. This path brings you to an old congregational chapel which is now used six times a year during the summer months. From the chapel, follow the farm track to Gyrnos, where there was a meadow for the overnight grazing of the cattle. From that farm follow the track south for Hirdir, and then turn left. If you keep always to the left along this road, you will come into Gwenddwr village by the post office. And so make your way to Erwood village.

The inn at Erwood was once a 'rendezvous for Dick Turpins', according to one of the local vicars, who recalled in the 1930s that, before the First World War, one of his churchwardens told him stories of the drovers being robbed by highwaymen at this ford. The old gentleman was almost eighty when he told these tales to the vicar, and he could remember as a lad helping to get the black cattle from Pembrokeshire across the Erwood ford. The inn does not boast of its Turpin past today, but it is slightly ironic that its patrons should be informed that its fame lies in the fact that it was here that Henry Mayhew wrote the short stories that were the origins of *Punch*. He was seeking refuge at Erwood from his London creditors at that time.

096431   Opposite the inn you will see a telephone box and some steps going up the bank between two cottages. If you climb up the narrow lane between these cottages and go through the gate at the end of it you will come to a track which leads up the hillside to the Twmpath. On your right, the lane descends steeply to the new bridge across the Wye at Erwood, which has been built over the site of the old ford. Do not follow this, but take the lane

066441   running north-west. It goes past the farm of Cefn-hirwaun and when it is crossed by another lane, turn right. After a mile (1.6 kilometres) along this lane you will come to a farm track on your left. Follow this, and once past the farm take the steep

The Wye ford at Erwood

climb on to the hill where you will find it is crossed by a track running east/west. Turn to the west here and continue over the hill, always walking in a westerly direction with Pwll-du (the black pool) on your right. This brings you on to the road just north of Cwm Owen. From there, if you have a car, you can go north for a little way and then take the first turn on your right for Erwood. The first left-hand turn off this lane is the way past Cefn-hirwaun, which you will have walked. From there you carry on down the hill, as the road winds steeply to the new bridge.

This road is known as the Twmpath. It is made up now, but the author of *The Trail of the Black Ox* relates that, 'The track was ploughed by the hoofs of the cattle in the damp weather, and manured by the cattle as they passed over it. In the dry weather it would be harrowed by the hoofs of the cattle again. No bracken or fern has grown on it since, and it is still today a green sward which has not been used since the black cattle went over it.'

You can still see something of what he meant on the hillside to the north of the lane between the farms of Groeswen and Cefngarth. This is where you would come out if you were to walk east from Pwll-du and keep round the side hill in a south-easterly direction. Some of the cattle would have been brought along this path, and even in a dry summer it still shows a clear green.

Lake Pwll-du

From the new bridge it is still quite easy to see the ford. The Wye is quite wide here, and its rock bed is made up of little ridges which would make a steady paving for the cattle. It must have been a dramatic sight to see the great herds cross the river. To quote *The Trail of the Black Ox* again, 'The guide would start to cross slowly blowing his horn. Dogs would be barking and the drovers shouting as the cattle start to follow the horse to the river. Many of the drovers would be in the water driving the cattle on.'

The crossing was even more dramatic when the Wye was in flood. Then the ferryman had to take the cattle over in his 'boat', a large wooden box, which was winched across the river on a chain. During the nineteenth century, in the last days of the drovers, the ferryman was notably short in stature and kept

the inn on the east bank of the river. John Lloyd (Breconshire's historian) imagines Little Tom (Twm Bach as the ferryman was known) like Charion at the River Styx, and suggests that he must often have prayed for rain to make the Wye unfordable.[26]

There is a sad ending to Little Tom's story, which Mr E. Jones of Crickhowell described in an article in *The Western Mail* of March 2nd, 1935. Little Tom 'was taking a boat-load of cattle over when the Wye was in flood, and the cattle in spite of the efforts of the two drovers in charge of them rushed to the side of the boat in terror of the down-coming flood of water and swamped the boat. The drovers saved themselves by clutching at the tails of the animals, and were towed ashore, but Little Tom and his son in their efforts to save the boat were drowned.'

094446

Having crossed the Wye, the cattle were taken to the shoeing station of Painscastle. From the bridge follow the road to the left as it runs along the east bank of the Wye, until you come to a lane on your right for the village of Llandeilo Graban. From there take the left-hand lane for Llewetrog, Llanbedr and Painscastle. The walks over Llanbedr Hill, following some of the tracks that would have been used in bringing the cattle down from the farms to the north, have been given in the preceding section.

Another alternative is to climb the hill to your right from Llanbedr, going in a north-easterly direction, and then descend the hill by the second track on your right. This brings you into Painscastle by the chapel at the side of the Maesllwch Arms, which once served as both inn and smithy, a common doubling of functions.

1946

From the shoeing stations at Painscastle, the cattle were taken over Clyro Hill to cross into England at Rhydspence. These old tracks have recently been made into roads, so that there can be proper communications between the outlying farms. But they are still lovely to walk along and in several places, especially as you go over Clyro Hill, you will see the wide verges – the only visible reminders that the cattle were once brought this way, and given time to graze as they went.

Painscastle ramparts

The whole area that lies between Painscastle and Newchurch to the north and Clyro and Rhydspence to the south bears such traces of the droves. It offers opportunities for numerous short walks along the lanes past historic mounds and old farm buildings, which were familiar to Francis Kilvert and which he often mentioned in his diaries. Even at that time the young curate of Clyro was nostalgic for the good old days of the drovers. On May 3rd, 1870, he took a walk over Clyro Hill towards Crowthers Pool, 'speculating upon the probable site of the Coldbrook and the Black Ox which was the house of call on Clyro Hill for the drovers of the great herds of black cattle from Shire Carmarthen and Cardigan on the way down into England.'

Francis Kilvert lived in Clyro for seven years, from the age of twenty-five to thirty-two (1865-72). He was innocent, often to the point of foolishness, immensely sociable, modest and kind. Like many another Victorian cleric, he was a keen and accurate observer of birds and wild flowers, and he had a greater gift than any of them for using his diaries to crystallize the delights he found in nature. He is still the best companion for a walker among these hills. A paperback selection of the diaries, edited by the late William Plomer, from which I have taken these quotations, was published by Jonathan Cape in 1964.

In 1903, John Lloyd of Brecon reported, 'At the present day, large flocks of sheep are taken to England along the old track, and that on Clyro Hill – although the hill has been enclosed, a broad open roadway has been left unenclosed, and which is known as the cattle track.'[27]

From the Black Ox, wherever on Clyro Hill its ruins must lie, the drovers came into Rhydspence; here they could choose between the Welsh inn on one side of the stream and the adjoining English inn, which was also a smithy, on the other. The Welsh inn is now a private house but the English one, now known as the Rhydspence Inn, is interesting both for its extreme old age (it was built about 1350) and for the old horse-operated cider press which stands in its yard and which was used until 1956. It is a good place to end the drove trails, and appropriately enough its present landlords, Peter and Pam Sharratt, came to the inn from Kent – the county for which the most adventurous of the drovers were bound.

Cider press at Rhydspence Inn

1   *Wild Wales* (J. M. Dent, London, 1958).
2   'Some Ardudwy Cattle Drovers', *Merioneth Journal*, January 1974.
3   Ibid.
4   *Wild Wales*, op. cit.
5   Ibid.
6   *The Rebecca Riots* (University of Wales Press, Cardiff, 1954).
7   Combridge, Birmingham, 1932.
8   *A Tour Through the Whole Island of Great Britain* (1724-6), vol. 2 (Penguin, Harmondsworth, 1971).
9   Faber, London, 1969.
10 *The Rebecca Riots*, op. cit.
11 Ibid.
12 *History of Radnorshire* (Scolar Press, London, 1973).
13 Ibid.
14 *Transactions of the Royal Historical Society,* 1971.
15 *History of Radnorshire*, op. cit.
16 *The Old Straight Track* (Sphere, London, 1974).
17 Ibid.
18 *The Welsh Cattle Drovers* (University of Wales Press, Cardiff, 1976).
19 *A Tour Through the Whole Island of Great Britain*, op. cit.
20 Edited by Sir John E. Lloyd for the London Carmarthenshire Society.
21 *Wild Wales*, op. cit.
22 *A Tour Through the Whole Island of Great Britain*, op. cit.
23 *Historical Memoranda of Breconshire*, 1903.
24 Ibid.
25 Ibid.
26 Ibid.
27 Ibid.

Part Four

Epilogue

The Drovers in England

GWAIR TYMHERUS – PORFA FLASUS – CWRW DA – A
CWAL CYSURUS

Years ago a Welshman – or a well-trained English inn-keeper –
painted these letters on the side of the Drovers' House, which
still stands on the west bank of the Test at Stockbridge, a
Hampshire town, just outside Winchester. The present owners
of the house keep the paint restored, so you can clearly read the
early advertisement for 'Worthwhile grass – pleasant pasture –
good beer – and – a comfortable shelter.'

From this village you can follow the old drove way north-east to
Preston Candover. This is the way that the drovers from South
Wales would have gone, on their way east to Farnham in Surrey
and through to Kent. They would probably have carried bales
of knitted garments with them for sale at the Farnham stocking
markets, which were held at Michaelmas and Christmas.
Their route went along the ancient Lunway, now covered by a
modern road, along a lane now officially known as the Alresford
Drove, and so to the footpath, officially marked on the
Ordnance Survey map as the Ox Drove Road. This route is
marked along its length by yew trees, which in this chalky soil
served the same purpose as the Scots pines of mid-Wales. They
acted as way marks to the drovers and indicated where food,
lodging and grazing might be had.

Some two miles (3.2 kilometres) south-west of Preston Candover you will pass by Bangor Wood, a little to the west of
Bugmore Hill. This was the site of a famous droving inn, now
demolished. The County Council has recently even filled up its
well. So now nothing remains except the strange name of the
area, the green pasture which still retains its lush fertility, and
the memory of a murder. It is a familiar story. The legend goes

that the inn was once owned by two brothers, one of whom slit the other's throat with a razor to get *all* the drovers' wealth. For the Welsh drovers, Bangor Inn was just a staging post on the journey. Many of them still had well over a hundred miles (160 kilometres) to go before they reached their destination in Kent. There the cattle were sold at Maidstone Fair, which was held during the first week in October, and at the cattle fairs of Canterbury, Chilham and Wingham.

The cattle that were taken through Gloucestershire were mostly on their way to the fattening pastures of the Vale of Aylesbury, and the Hertfordshire fairs. For a long stretch of the way the drove went along the Roman road of Ermine Street. One of the most dramatic parts of the journey began at the village of Great Witcombe, some five miles (eight kilometres) east of Gloucester. After they had been shod in what is now the Roseville forge in that village, the cattle were driven along the footpath which leaves the highway on its northern side. This action was taken in order to avoid the toll gate, which had to charge heavy dues in order to keep up the difficult stretch of road, with its one in six gradient on the eastern side of Birdlip Hill. You can still follow their route along that path to Hill Farm, from where it makes the hazardous steep descent back to the main road.

For centuries the main trade was with Kent. By the sixteenth century the long summer drove from North Wales to that distant English county was part of the rhythm of agricultural life. The drovers of those days expected to spend about three weeks on their 250 mile (402 kilometres) journey.

By the eighteenth century the route was so established that it was quite usual for the drovers' dogs to make their own way home again. One of these dogs is known to us by name. Cailo belonged to a drover from Llandrillo to the south-west of Corwen. When his master reached Kent, he put his pony's saddle on the dog's back, and pointed his nose towards the west. He had prepared for his dog's return journey by asking every innkeeper he had stayed with on his way to the east to feed and rest the animal on its solitary return. In common with usual practice, the pony was sold to an English buyer. That habit persisted even after the coming of the railways, when it was quite usual for a pony to be sent with the cattle or sheep. It was used by the drover who took the animals from the station to their English grazing lands, then sold to an English buyer.

Infectious sickness among the cattle – whether it was known as murrain, pestilence or plague – was one of the worst disasters that could hit the drovers. The middle years of the eighteenth century were particularly disastrous. Between 1745 and 1759 half a million cattle perished in recurring outbreaks of rinderpest, and many of the drovers suffered substantial losses. In 1747 and 1748 the October fair at Chilham in Kent was cancelled; and in the latter year arrangements were made for 'Eight Welch gentlemen' with 616 runts to be segregated in near-by Eastwell Park, which was used as a quarantine area. An article by Dennis Baker in *The Journal of the Merioneth Historical Society* for 1972, entitled 'An Eighteenth-century Cattle Drover', led me to look up the amounts of compensation that some of these Welshmen received from the Kent authorities during the plague years. On January 15th, 1754, the drover William Rowland from Tan-y-bwlch near Maentwrog, who is mentioned in the Porthmadog section of this book, received £12 for the loss of his 'distempered horned cattle'. He had driven eighty-four beasts to the Kent fairs that year.

By the nineteenth century the drovers, like many other people in the British Isles, had realized that there were pickings to be made out of the Napoleonic Wars. Professor Skeel records the tale told by a lad who helped to shoe the cattle at Abergwili Fair, who had done some work for a drover taking cattle into Kent in 1809 and 1810 for the sole purpose of smuggling them into France.[1] It would be interesting to know what he got from that illegal sale, for presumably it was a far more profitable transaction than selling beasts on the open market.

In the bar of the King's Head at Llandovery you can read a letter from Thomas Evans, a drover of that region, which tells you what the legal nineteenth-century Kent prices were. Evans's letter, which he wrote from Ashford on April 16th, 182? quotes a top price of £7, and only one animal realized that – £5 10 seems to have been the usual amount.

It is interesting that the drovers who went to Kent were also familiar figures at the Hertfordshire fairs. Those who were going direct from Wales to Barnet would have gone through the south Midlands to the Buckinghamshire grazing lands. In May 1925, when she was eighty-eight, the niece of a former landlord of the New Inn at Padbury remembered what it was like when the Welsh drovers came. Professor Skeel got the story at second-hand, but it seems authentic.

Mr Webb the landlord was always anxious that the drovers should put up at his inn, and his niece was impressed by 'their large droves of cattle and little Welsh mountain sheep, which no fence could keep in'. Yet somehow the animals were secured, and the drovers came into the inn for a large supper. But they didn't enter the building before the landlord's houseproud wife had taken wise precautions. When she learnt that the drovers were on their way, she took up the carpet in the bedroom and threw the curtains on to the top of the four poster bed.

Many of the nineteenth-century drovers going through Buckinghamshire were on their way to Barnet Fair, which is still held in the first week of September each year. Welsh cattle were known in that county from the fifteenth century. Others were going further east, to Epping and Billericay. The descendant of one drover lives in retirement in Thame, at the southern end of the rich lands of the vale of Aylesbury.

Mr Morris Roberts spent many years dealing in sheep and cattle before he settled down a farmer, first in Kent and then in Buckinghamshire. Throughout the 1920s he bought cattle and sheep in his native Wales and brought them through to Essex. He was the youngest of three brothers, and was born at the turn of the century at the family farm of Hendre Mawr, about two miles (3.2 kilometres) out of Bala on the Trawsfynydd road. His sister still lives at the farm of Ciltalgarth to the east of Llyn Celyn. Both she and her brother can remember that valley before it was flooded to supply Liverpool's water; and as a young man, Mr Roberts bought cattle from the farms that now lie drowned there.

For generations cattle dealing and droving was a family tradition. A great uncle, another Morris Roberts, was a very important sheep dealer in Gwyddelwern, and his father walked cattle all the way into England during the First World War, when the trains were needed for the troops.

Young Mr Roberts didn't take to so much walking; although even when the railways were fully geared to the transportation of livestock, a certain amount was inevitable. One way and another, before he eventually settled down to farm, Mr Roberts spent most of his working life on the road, either on foot or, being an early motorist, in his Ford car.

For the most part, he bought the cattle direct from the farms. To do so he went as far as Dolgellau to the west, Denbigh to the north and Welshpool to the east. He also bought cattle from the traditional droving centres of Pentrefoelas and Cerrigydrudion, and those he walked along the A5 to the railway at Corwen. At that time it was still the sort of road that the nineteenth-century drovers and George Borrow would have known. Despite the very occasional car, the road was not made up, and for most of the year it was simply a muddy track.

At Corwen the cattle were put on the train for Waltham Cross; and with them went the money to pay Mr Cook, the Essex drover. He met the beasts and walked them through Epping Forest to Chelmsford. In the late 1920s he charged a £1 a day. Mr Roberts came on by car to see that everything went smoothly. It didn't always. Once he had to take fifty beasts single-handed through the forest ('It was all right so long as I just went nice and quiet,' he says).

Mr Roberts dealt mostly in shorthorns, but sometimes he would trade with Welsh blacks – 'They picked up wonderfully in two or three days,' he recalled. The most anxious time was the drought summer of 1921; but the situation was saved when the Essex drover suggested that he pastured his cattle on the salt marshes of Burnham on Crouch. It was successful.

In the 1930s, Mr Roberts gave up his nomadic life. He became a farmer, took a wife and raised a family. But although it was an inevitable decision, he still regrets that he had to make that break with the tradition of his ancestors.

1   *Transactions of the Royal Historical Society,* 1926.

Preparations for Walking

Builth Wells Market

Any long journey involves difficulties and dangers. The greatest hazards that the drovers had to face came from the violence arising out of human greed. They were carrying a lot of cash through very poor country, so they had to be constantly on the look-out for robbers who might be lying in ambush for them among the rocks and trees. Nor could they feel altogether secure with each other. Fratricide was not unknown, though it was rare and shocking enough for tales of it to persist over the centuries.

Yet in one respect the drovers were safer than the people who walk over these deserted tracks today: they knew their countryside as no visitor can ever hope to. With an almost instinctive knowledge passed on through the generations, they would know which marshy ground was pocketed with treacherous bogs, where the paths turn sharply by sudden precipices and how to find their way when sudden clouds engulf the uplands. Above all, they always travelled in large groups. To contrast their working journey with that of today's walkers is rather like noting the different conditions faced by the men who sailed the tea clippers and a pair of yachtsmen sailing a modern fibre-glass vessel. The image is not so fanciful, for setting out across hill country is much like going to sea. In both cases one has to respect wind and weather, and plan to survive in comfort among natural forces that are not going to bend to your needs. Both ocean and mountain can look deceptively safe and welcoming on a clear sunny day. But don't be fooled. Clouds come down swiftly out of blue sky and unless you are prepared you will lose your way; and on the heights the temperature drops steeply whenever the sun goes in. This needn't be too daunting, but there is always the chance that you may sprain or break an ankle some four or five miles (six to eight kilometres) across hill country from any human help. So it is proper to treat the expedition seriously, and to observe the general safety rules for hill-walkers.

1.　Do not set out alone without letting someone know what direction you are going in. It is best to do this even if you have a companion.

2.　Wear proper walking boots. Boots prevent slipping, support your ankles, and are essential for crossing streams and walking over marshy ground. Although some experienced walkers advocate stout plimsolls instead of boots, they obviously cannot give you the same sort of support. The really important thing is to avoid leather soles, which could be dangerous on many of these walks.

3.　Take a jersey even on the hottest day, and a light waterproof wind-cheater. It's a good idea to choose these in bright colours, which are easily visible should you get lost. The waterproofed nylon smocks intended for sailing are good garments and light to carry.

4.　Don't try to take too much food with you, although it is important to have something in case you get stranded. I favour oranges, because they don't get damaged in a rucksack, can't mark the maps and provide both moisture and sugar in a fairly compact and concentrated form.

5.　Take a compass, so that when the mists come down, you can defeat the natural tendency of the human animal to walk in circles. You will also find a compass essential when the way goes through pine forests, a hazard that the drovers did not have to face. In these new plantations there is absolutely nothing to distinguish one path or road from another, and, once you lose the sun, nothing to give you any indication as to the way you are heading. Sometimes your problem is to find out where you are, rather than decide which direction you want to head in. When that happens, a pocket barometer/altimeter is invaluable. If you know what height you are at, you can usually pinpoint your position pretty accurately; and the barometer will warn you of any abrupt changes in the weather.

6.　I have found a stick helpful, partly because it really is a support on long climbs. Its more essential function is to act as a probe to test out which hillocks on marshy ground are safe to walk on, and which will sink you waist deep in bog. Always treat marshland with respect. It is indicated by reeds, vivid green mosses and the pretty white wisps of bog cotton. On rocky uplands, where water cannot drain away, the bog can accumulate to a depth that would drown a man or horse.

7.   Take a small pocket torch in case you get benighted, although if you plan your route carefully allowing a speed of two miles an hour this shouldn't happen. Remember that six is the agreed emergency signal for anyone in trouble – six flashes of the torch, six blasts on a whistle.

Up to the seventeenth century, the drovers had to look out for wolves. The most ferocious wild animal you are likely to encounter is a wasp. It is the farm livestock that are most likely to cause you trouble. In Powys, as I have already noted, the farmers are exempt from the law which insists that bulls be kept off public footpaths; but as they are always running with the cows, they are not likely to be interested in a few walkers. A company of hikers might be another matter. Bulls can't see colours, so there's no need to take off your red anorak; but any sudden noise or wild movements may disturb them. So walk quietly and deliberately over any hillside where you have reason to think that a bull may be grazing.

Much more dangerous are cows with young calves and mares with foals. The protective maternal instinct can take quite an aggressive form in these animals, and it's best to keep right out of their way.

Welsh farm dogs, the ubiquitous black and white collies, can be a bother. Their bark luckily is a good deal worse than their bite, and most of them are fair cowards at heart. If you adopt a proper 'I'm lord of creation around here' stance and tone, show them your stick and say 'Pied' firmly and clearly, you will be astonished how they slink away. ('Pied', as in 'Pied Piper', simply means 'Stop'.) These dogs' lives are ruled by their sense of territory, and once you are clear of the land they have set themselves to defend you will hear no more of them. Whatever you do, do not run away. Even if the dogs should nip at your calves, do not regard that as a serious attack. 'It doesn't bite; it nobbut nips' – as the Yorkshire lady, quoted by W. R. Mitchell in *Wild Pennines*,[1] consoled the fell walker who was foolish enough to be scared of a barking dog. The dogs have been trained for generations to herd sheep and to tidy things away, and a fleeing human soon comes into that category. Always remember that these dogs are much loved and very valuable working animals. They may annòy you, but you are most unlikely to be harmed by them.

The dogs' territorial instinct is something that their owners share. Welsh farmers are as harassed as any others, and their friendliness and Celtic ability to turn any chance encounter into a party should not blind you to the fact that walkers are not unreservedly welcome. The farmers fear that gates will be left open, hay and crops trampled on, fences broken, sheep worried by dogs and livestock generally disturbed. This concern extends beyond the home fields, for the mountain grazing land is not common ground as it would be in England. There is no common land as such in Wales. The grazing rights are simply held in common by the surrounding farmers, who pay rent to the ground landlord (frequently one of the big city companies).

To ease the farmers' fears of walkers, always leave gates exactly as you find them. It can be quite annoying for the farmer who has deliberately opened a gate to find that some busybody has closed it. And if you have a dog with you see that it is properly under control. If it worries sheep you have no redress if it is shot. All this, together with the obvious injunction not to leave litter about, is simply a matter of the usual country code. Yet there are deeper implications.

Although you can still get there without a passport Wales, for any sensitive *Sais*, is distinctly abroad. The most tangible sign of this is the amount of Welsh you hear spoken. Although some country school teachers complain that there are few 'hearth-Welsh' children coming into their schools, the use of the language is increasing year by year. When you go abroad it is important to remember that you're the foreigner. So it is here. But if you can manage that, you will certainly learn more about the Welsh people, their landscape and their history than you would ever do if you simply treat it as another English county. As well as being a foreigner you are a tourist, in places where tourism is frequently the major industry. That can have disadvantages. You will sometimes have to share the mountain roads with the sightseers in their cars; and you will find that many small villages (such as Llangurig) have been dominated by 'craft' shops full of dull and mass-produced objects designed to meet an unthinking demand.

The advantage is that you'll have no difficulty at all in finding overnight accommodation, although in August it's wise to make your arrangements fairly early in the evening. You can camp almost anywhere, but the fact that there is no public common land means that it is only courteous to inform the farmer, who will probably charge a small fee of some 5p a night. There are several conveniently placed youth hostels near the drove routes; many farms offer a very good bed and breakfast at reasonable terms; and you may even like to spend a night in one of the old drovers' inns that can still offer accommodation.

Ways of agriculture over the centuries affect ways of society. Because there was never any feudal system in Wales, there are no traces of the class system that still inhibits so much life in England. It means that strangers, even 'tourists and foreigners', will never be regarded with sour suspicion, to be tolerated only for their pocket books. Happily, the Welsh love talking. This book can only give you the framework of the history that will come alive in conversation with men and women whose ancestors drove cattle and sheep from this foreign land through the Cotswolds into Kent and East Anglia.

1   Robert Hale, London, 1976

Welsh Words

The Welsh words that are relevant to this book are those that are connected with names of places. This is so because Welsh place names always have an immediate meaning that is closely related to the geographical, and very occasionally to the historical, significance of the area. Thus the ubiquitous *llan* signifies church or parish, and applies to a wide area of land which need not necessarily be inhabited. The syllable is always attached to the name of the saint who is supposed to have founded the church. Thus *Llangurig* means the parish surrounding the church founded by St Gurig.

A few basic rules of pronunciation will help you with these place names.

C is always hard. Like English K.
Dd is like the English Th in The. D is like English D.
F as in English V (there is no V in Welsh). Ff as in English F.
G is always hard as in Give.
Ll is almost like the English Th in This, with an L sound added to it. So Thl.
U is like the English short i in Pin, except at the end of a word when it becomes a double 'ee'. In place names you will usually find it in the suffix meaning black. So Llyn Du, pronounced Thlin dee, means the black lake. Bontddu, pronounced Bont thee, means the black bridge. The change in the form of the adjective is due to the gender of the noun it qualifies. Dee is the masculine form.
W is like the English long oo as in Look.
Y at the beginning and end of the word is pronounced like the English short i. In the middle of a word like the English short u.

Vocabulary

Aber = estuary, confluence
Afon = river
Allt = height or hill

Bach = small
Bala = outlet of a river or stream
Ban (pl. Bannau) = mountain
Bangor = monastery
Bedd (pl. Beddau) = grave
Betws = oratory or hermitage
Beudy = cowshed, byre
Blaen (pl. Blaenau) = head of a valley
Bod = dwelling
Bont (also Pont) = bridge
Bran = crow
Bron = hill top
Buarth = cattle fold
Bugail = shepherd
Bwlch (pl. Bylchau) = mountain pass

Caban = hut
Cae = field
Caer = fort, encampment
Capel = chapel
Carreg (pl. Cerrig) = rock
Cefn = ridge, path
Clawdd = bank or dyke
Clun = meadow
Clwyd = gate
Coch = red
Coed (pl. Coedydd) = woodland
Corlan = sheep fold
Cors = bog
Craig = rock
Cwm = valley

Ddol = meadow
Ddu = black
Ddwr = water
Diffwys = a precipice
Dinas = fort
Diserth = a hermitage, retreat
Dyffryn = a valley

Efail = smithy
Eglwys = church
Eppynt = horse track
Erw = acre
Esgair = ridge

Fan = place, height
Fawn (Mawn) = peat
Felin (Melin) = mill
Ffair = fair, market place
Ffordd = road
Ffos = ditch
Ffridd = mountain pasture
Ffrwd = waterfall
Ffynnon = spring, well
Foel (Moel) = bare hill

Garth = enclosed hill
Gwaun = moor

Haf = summer
Hafod = summer dwelling
Hen = old
Hendre = winter dwelling
Heol = road
Hir = long

Is = below
Isaf = lowest

Llan = parish
Llety = shelter, lodging
Llwybr = path
Llyn = lake

Maen (pl. Meini) = stone
Maes = open field
Melin (Felin) = mill
Mign = bog
Migneint = boggy hollows
Mynydd = mountain

Nant = stream/valley
Neuadd = hall
Newydd = new

Ogof = cave

Pandy = fulling mill
Pant = valley
Pen = top
Pentref = village
Pistyll = waterfall
Plas = mansion
Porth = port, gateway
Pren = wood
Pwll = pool

'r = the, of the
Rhaeadr = waterfall

Rhiw = hill
Rhos = marshy moor
Rhyd = ford

Sais = English
Sarn = paved road

Tafarn = tavern
Tir = land
Tre/tref = hamlet
Twll = hole
Twmp, twmpath = mound
Ty = house
Tyddyn = small holding

Uchaf = highest

Waun (Gwaun) = moor
Wern (Gwern) = bog, marsh

Ysbyty = hospice, hospital
Ystrad = valley floor

Bibliography

The last wave of interest in the Welsh drovers took place in the 1920s and 1930s. Much of the background material for this book was taken from newspaper articles (appearing chiefly in the *Western Daily Mail* during the mid-1930s) and from papers published in academic journals.

The main books on droving currently in print are K. J. Bonser's *The Drovers* (Macmillan, London, 1970), which concentrates mainly on the Scottish droves, and Dr Richard Colyer's *The Welsh Cattle Drovers* (University of Wales Press, Cardiff, 1976).

For a general background to the social history of the farming communities in Wales, turn to J. Geraint Jenkin's *Life and Tradition in Rural Wales* (Dent, London, 1976). Mr Jenkins is Keeper of the Department of Material Culture at the Welsh Folk Museum of St Fagans, near Cardiff.

A more specific aspect of that history is given in David Williams's *The Rebecca Riots* (University of Wales Press, Cardiff, 1954) which gives an account of the toll-gate riots of the 1830s and 1840s. These are dealt with in fictional form in Alexander Cordell's *Hosts of Rebecca* (Pan, London, 1970).

The very best history of the Welsh drovers is now sadly out of print. It is P. G. Hughes's *Wales and the Drovers* and it was published in Evans Social Studies series in 1947. It is not easily available, but among the institutions which do hold a copy is the Kent Education Committee.

There are one or two novels based on the drovers, the best of these being Roy Saunders's *The Drovers Highway* and Richard Vaughan's *Who Rideth so Wild*, but these are both unfortunately out of print. Elizabeth Clarke's *The Valley* (Faber, London, 1969), which is a fictional account of life on a Radnorshire hill-farm in the early years of this century, is easily available.

George Borrow's *Wild Wales* is still the best companion to any tour of that country, and I advise the 1958 Everyman edition. And because Borrow would shame anybody who sets foot in Wales without poems in his head, I would recommend almost any volume of R. S. Thomas's work. His publishers are Hart-Davis MacGibbon.

Index

Abbeycwmhir 25, 142, 153, 166, 169-170
Aberdaron 50
Aberedw Hill 181, 182, 185, 187
Abergwesyn 150, 152, 171, 191
Aberystwyth 11, 151, 152
Agriculture, Board of 17
Albert Mount 207
Allinson, Martin 116
Anglesey 9, 49-50
Ardudwy 10, 91, 113
Arthur, King 28, 103

Bala 10, 30, 78, 91, 118, 123-124, 227
Bangor Inn (Hampshire) 225
Banking 13, 16, 151-152, 210
Barn (Cwmyrychen) 168
Barnet Fair 227
Berwyn 125, 128, 130
Bettws Gwerfil Goch 81
Beulah 171, 172, 181, 191
Birmingham Water Corporation 150
Blaenau Ffestiniog 60, 65
Blaen-Cothi 199, 200
Blaen-Twrch 199
Blaenycwm 153, 154
Bodtalog 154, 155, 165
Bogs 44, 230-231
Bontddu 99, 110
Boots (walking) 230
Borrow, George 20, 50, 80, 85, 91, 135, 154, 181, 210
Bowen E. G. 10, 11
Brecon 191, 211
Brecon Beacons 150, 214
Brecon Museum 124, 213

Bright, John 138
Bron-y-foel 97, 103, 105
Builth Wells 14, 150, 170, 176, 177, 179, 181, 191, 216
Bulkeley, William 49
Bulls 212, 231
Burial Sites 27, 96

Caeo 9, 207
Caersws 143
Cairns 27, 115, 116, 134, 195
Cambrian forge 151
Camping 26, 233
Cattle, breeds of 16
Cattle pens 31
Cattle plague 226
Cefn Cardis 171, 172
Ceiriog 130
Cellan 195
Celts 136
Cerrigydrudion 79, 80, 81, 228
Chapels 200
Charles, Thomas 124
Chartists 143
Churches 27
Churchyards (circular) 27
Cider 19
Cilycwm 194, 195, 199, 202, 209
Civil War 12, 85, 200
Claerwen Reservoir 158, 164
Clark, John 33, 211, 212
Clarke, Elizabeth 164, 165
Clothes (drovers) 10
Clyro 151, 186, 221
Cnicht 60
Cobden, Richard 138
Colva 179, 187
Colyer, Richard 9, 15, 21, 191

Compass 230
Corwen 125, 130, 228
Cows 231
Craig Goch Reservoir 158
Cregrina 182, 185, 187
Criccieth 51
Crickadarn 217
Croesor 60-65
Cues 20
Curig (saint) 137
Cwm Bychan 97, 115
Cwm Nantcol 93, 97-98, 116
Cwm Owen 217, 219
Cwmystwyth 137, 152
Cwrt-y-Cadno 200
Cynghordy 209
Cynwyd 128

Dafydd, Sion 80
Davies, John (dealer) 213
Davies, Jonathan (drover) 14
Davies, Walter 25
Dee 125
Defoe, Daniel 159
Denbigh 81, 228
Devil's Bridge 137, 152, 155, 161
Disserth 176
Dogs 38
Dogs, Collie 231-232
Dogs, Corgi 10, 225
Dolaucothi 194
Dolbenmaen Range 53, 115
Dolgellau 15, 30, 91, 110-112, 118, 228
Dolhelfa 166
Dolwyddelan 67
Druid 128
Dyffryn Ardudwy 93